Sight
for
Sound

Sight for Sound
DESIGN & MUSIC MIXES +

General Editor:
Roger Walton

Sight for Sound

First published in paperback in
1998 by Hearst Books International
1350 Avenue of the Americas
New York, NY 10019
United States of America

Distributed in the United States
and Canada by
Watson-Guptill Publications
1515 Broadway
New York, NY 10036

Distributed in Germany,
Switzerland, Austria, and
Scandinavia by
Gingko Press GmbH
Hamburger Strasse 180
D-22083 Hamburg, Germany
Tel: (040) 291-425
Fax: (040) 291-055

Distributed throughout the
rest of the world by
Hearst Books International
1350 Avenue of the Americas
New York, NY 10019

ISBN 0-688-16454-4

Edited and Designed by
Duncan Baird Publishers
Castle House
75-76 Wells Street
London W1P 3RE

Managing Designer:
Gabriella Le Grazie
Designer: Richard Horsford
Editor: Ingrid Court-Jones
Researcher: Max Bielenberg

Commissioned artwork (pages 1-9,
84-5): Lopetz97, courtesy of
büro destruct, Berne

10 9 8 7 6 5 4 3 2 1

Typeset in Bank Gothic BT and
Letter Gothic MT
Color reproduction by Colourscan,
Singapore
Printed in Hong Kong

KEY TO SYMBOLS USED IN CAPTIONS

A Art Director
D Designer(s): Design company
✪ Title: Artist
● Record label/client
P Photographer(s)
I Illustrator
■ Description and dimensions*
✈ Country of origin

*NOTE
All CD covers, booklets, fold-out
concertinas, cases, and packages
are a standard size of 120 x 120
mm (4¾ x 4¾ in) unless otherwise
specified. All album sleeves are
a standard size of 305 x 305 mm
(12 x 12 in).

CONTENTS

FOREWORD

Sight for Sound is a collection of printed design work specifically produced for the music business. Gathered from a wide range of sources, it seeks to illustrate the high quality of contemporary design for music as diverse as classical and easy listening, hardcore techno, and acid jazz.

The collection features CDs, CD covers and booklets, vinyl - both singles and albums - magazines and advertising posters, as well as flyers, badges, and stickers. The book is divided into two parts: the first, *Mix 1 - various artists*, brings together designs for many different musical forms; the second section, *Mix 2 - club mix,* is largely inspired by and generated for the club scene.

With the rise in popularity of the CD, designers have been forced to work with a much smaller format than that of the record sleeve, obliging them to find new design styles and techniques. This challenge has produced an ingenious array of design solutions, including the use of concertina fold-out covers to dramatically increase the space available for both graphics and text, and the utilization of unusual materials for the CD case, such as tinted plastic, tin, and cloth, as well as various types of paper and card.

Although the CD is currently the prevailing format, other products, such as cassette tapes and 7in, 10in, and 12in vinyl records, are still widely available. Consequently, designers are now often faced with the task of producing type and images which work for all these formats, and which also have international appeal.

As music promotion seeks to exploit an ever-increasing range of products and markets, the scope for innovation is immense. The sheer diversity of design has never been greater, nor the overall quality higher than it is today - as this inspiring collection clearly reveals.

RW

KEY TO SYMBOLS USED IN CAPTIONS

▲ Art Director
▣ Designer(s): Design company
✿ Title: Artist
● Record label/client
▣ Photographer(s)
▮ Illustrator
■ Description and dimensions*
✈ Country of origin

*NOTE
All CD covers, booklets, fold-out
concertinas, cases, and packages
are a standard size of 120 x 120 mm
(4¾ x 4¾ in) unless otherwise
specified. All album sleeves are
a standard size of 305 x 305 mm
(12 x 12 in).

8

mix
various artists

❶ **❷**

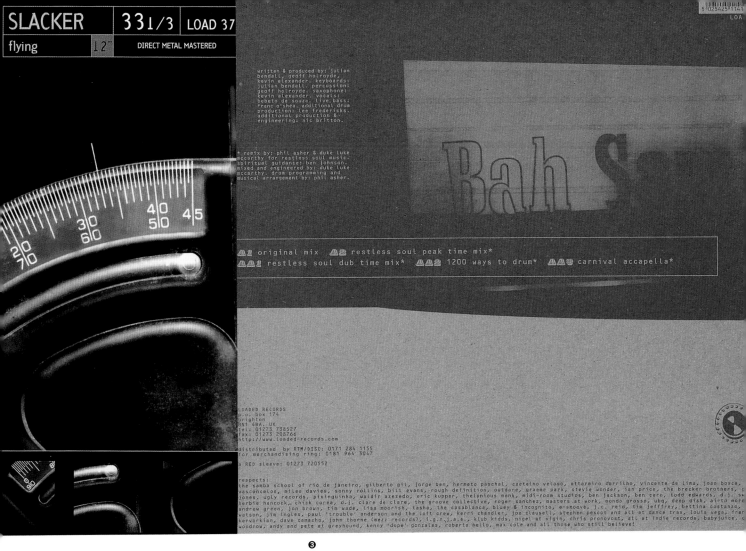

SLACKER   33 1/3   LOAD 37

flying   12"   DIRECT METAL MASTERED

written & produced by: julian
bendall, geoff holroyde,
kevin alexander. keyboards:
julian bendall. percussion:
geoff holroyde. saxophone:
kevin alexander. vocals:
bebeto de souza. live bass:
franc o'shea. additional drum
production: lee fredericks.
additional production &
engineering: nic britton.

* remix by: phil asher & duke luke
mccarthy for restless soul music.
spiritual guidance: ben johnson.
mixed and engineered by: duke luke
mccarthy. drum programming and
musical arrangement by: phil asher.

△1 original mix   △2 restless soul peak time mix*
△△1 restless soul dub time mix*   △△2 1200 ways to drum*   △△3 carnival accapella*

loaded records
p.o. box 174
brighton
BN1 4BA. UK
tel: 01273 738527
fax: 01273 208766
http://www.loaded-records.com

distributed by RTM/DISC: 0171 284 1155
for merchandising ring: 0181 964 3047

a RED sleeve: 01273 720552

respects:
the samba school of rio de janeiro, gilberto gil, jorge ben, hermeto paschal, caetaino veloso, attarmiro carrilho, vincente de lima, joao bosca,
vasconcelos, miles davies, sonny rollins, bill evans, rough definition, outdare, graeme park, stevie wonder, ian price, the brecker brothers, c
jones, ugly records, pixinguinha, waldir azezedo, eric kupper, thelonious monk, midi-room studios, ben jackson, ben caro, todd edwards, d.j. sw
herbie hancock, chick corea, d.j. clare de clare, the groove collective, roger sanchez, masters at work, mondo grosso, ubq, deep dish, airto more
andrew green, jon brown, tim wade, lisa moorish, tasha, the casablanca, bluey & incognito, e-smoove, j.c. reid, tim jefffrey, bettina costanzo,
watson, jim ingles, paul 'trouble' anderson and the loft crew, kerri chandler, joe clausell, stephen pescot and all at dance trax, louis vega, fran
kervorkian, dave camacho, john thorne (mezz records), i.g.n.j.a.e., klub kidds, nigel at virgin, chris pronovost, all at indie records, babyjuice, c
woodrow, andy and pete at greyhound, kenny 'dope' gonzales, roberto mello, max cole and all those who still believe!

❸

❹

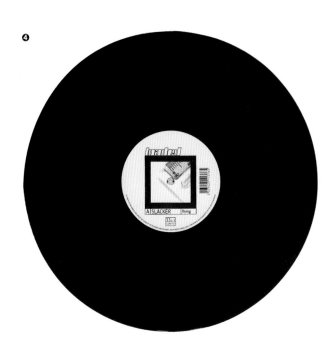

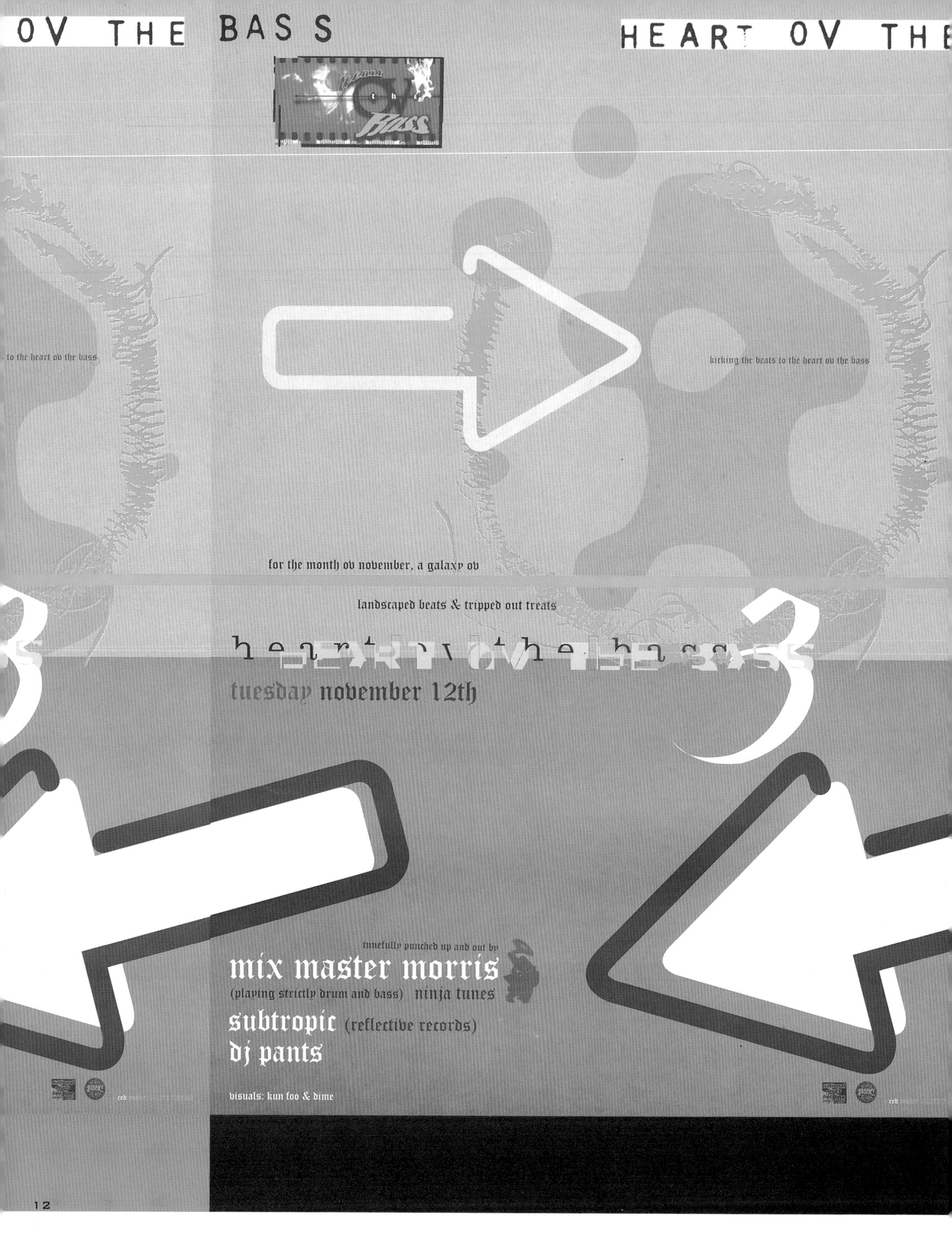

to the heart ov the bass

kicking the beats to the heart ov the bass

for the month ov november, a galaxy ov

landscaped beats & tripped out treats

heart ov the bass

tuesday november 12th

tunefully punched up and out by

mix master morris

(playing strictly drum and bass) ninja tunes

subtropic (reflective records)

dj pants

visuals: kun foo & dime

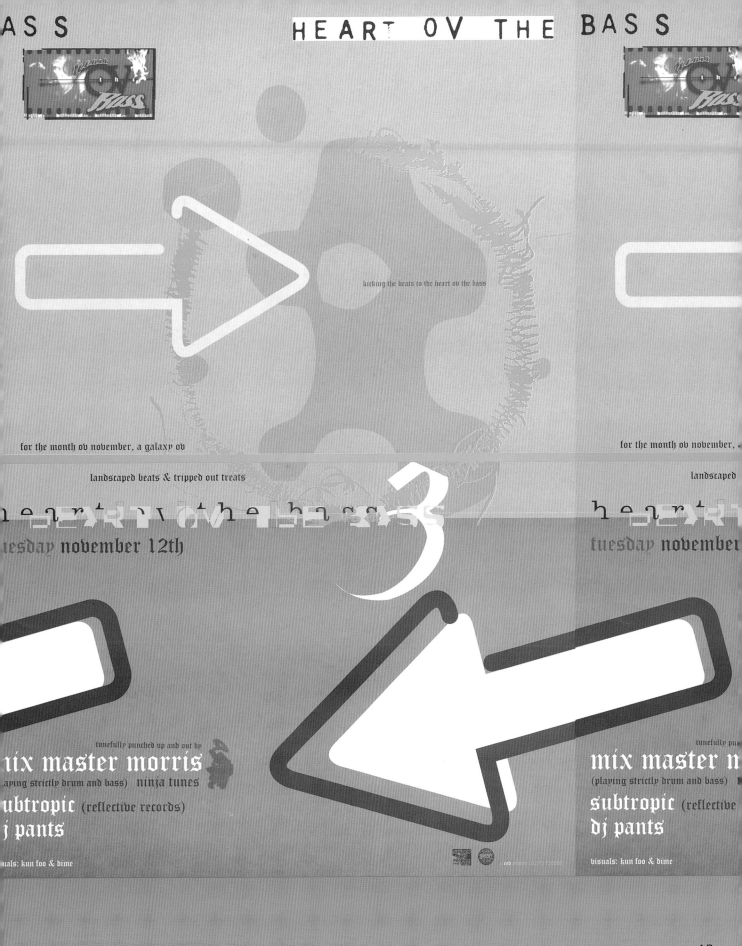

kicking the beats to the heart ov the bass

for the month ov november, a galaxy ov

for the month ov november,

landscaped beats & tripped out treats

landscaped

heart ov the bass

tuesday november 12th

tuesday november

tunefully punched up and out by

tunefully pu

mix master morris

mix master n

(playing strictly drum and bass)   **ninja tunes**

(playing strictly drum and bass)

ubtropic (reflective records)

subtropic (reflective

j pants

dj pants

uals: kun foo & dime

visuals: kun foo & dime

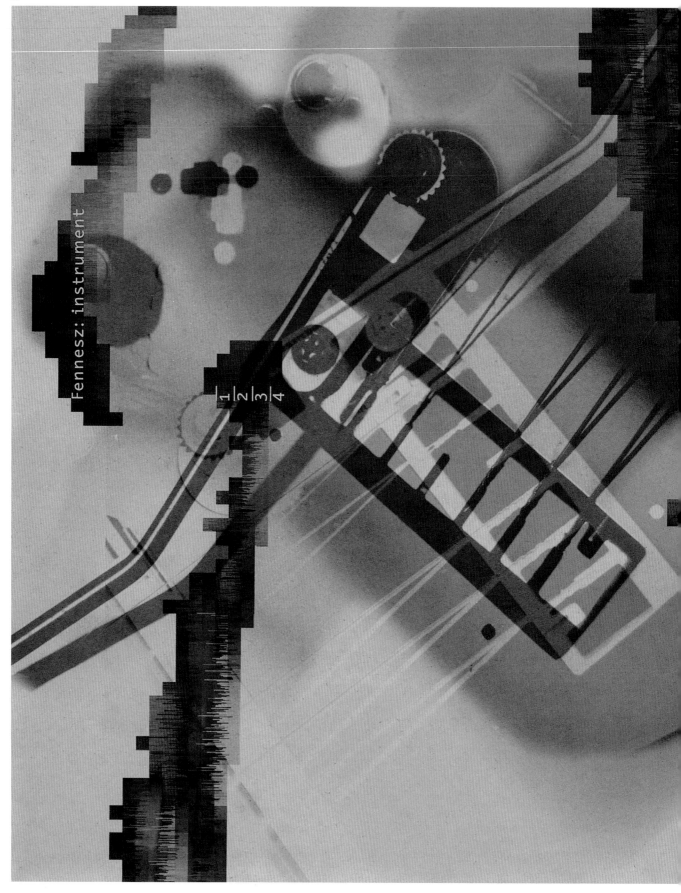

Fennesz: instrument

1 2 3 4

Pita: SEVEN TONS FOR FREE

mego 009

D TINA FRANK:
INWIREMENTS

● MEGO

P TINA FRANK

❶ ✪ INSTRUMENT:
FENNESZ

■ ALBUM SLEEVE

❷ ✪ SEVEN TONS FOR FREE:
PITA

■ CD PACKAGE
140 X 165 MM
5 ½ X 6 ½ IN

✈ AUSTRIA

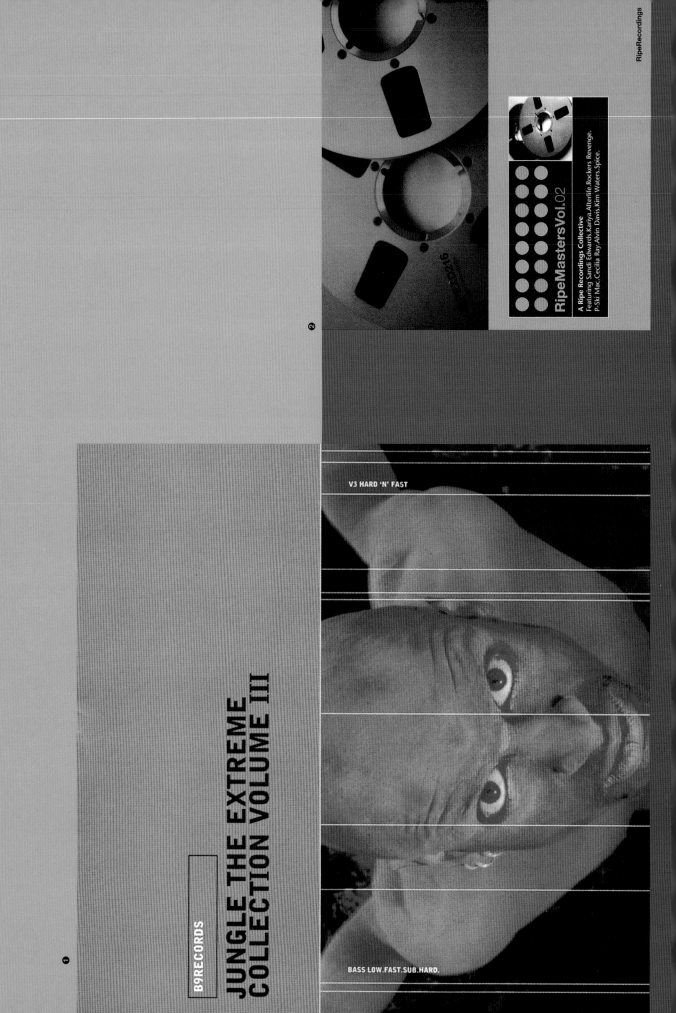

B9RECORDS

JUNGLE THE EXTREME
COLLECTION VOLUME III

V3 HARD 'N' FAST

BASS LOW.FAST.SUB.HARD.

RipeMastersVol.02

A Ripe Recordings Collective
Featuring Sandi Edwards.Kariya.Afterlife.Rockers Revenge.
P-Ski Mac.Cecilia Ray.Alvin Davis.Kim Waters.Spice.

RipeRecordings

Isabella Bordoni
Roberto Paci Dalò

many many voices

the listening room:

edel

MOSS TALES

David Moss

the listening room:

1 Vicenza 2 Ghent 3 Australia 4 Woody & Heiner 5 Africa 6 Italian Private Party 7 Russian Story 8 Bahia, Brazil 9 Berlin Tale 10 Vicenza 11 Australia 12 Woody & Heiner 13 Africa 14 Russian Story 15 Berlin Tale

edel 0041502TLR
Made in Germany by optimal

MOSS TALES surprised me, almost from the beginning! I really had no idea I could do this: play, sing, speak (half Deutsch, half English), tell stories and make music at the same time - improvising - with my memory of these funny experiences as my only safety net. The idea came from Manfred Mixner, chief of the Hörspiel Department at SFB radio in Berlin. He heard me perform in Roberto Paci Dalò's Many Many Voices' and he seemed to know that I had lots of voices and stories to tell – and asked me to think about the idea. So I went home and made a list of some of the wild experiences I've had at my concerts, in my travels, with artists and audiences around the world. My original list totaled 29 strange events. Then one morning in April 1995 I went to the SFB studios and set up my instruments (drums, electronics amplified objects) and we sound-checked I looked at my list and picked these nine tales. I began to play and sing and talk. It's a funny world!

Fast von Anfang an waren MOSS TALES eine Überraschung für mich. Ich hatte wirklich keine Ahnung, daß ich so etwas könnte: spielen, singen, sprechen (halb Deutsch-halb Englisch), im gleichen Moment Geschichten erzählen und Musik machen (improvisieren), mit meiner Erinnerung an diese witzigen Erlebnisse als einziger Sicherheit.
Manfred Mixner, Chef der Hörspielabteilung des Sender Freies Berlin, hatte die Idee hierzu. Er hörte mich auf einer Aufnahme von Roberto Paci Dalòs Many Many Voices' und schien sofort zu wissen, daß ich noch viele Stimmen und Geschichten zur Verfügung hatte - und bat mich über die Idee nachzudenken. Ich fuhr also Heim und stellte eine Liste von außergewöhnlichen Erlebnissen zusammen, die ich auf meinen Konzerten, Reisen, mit Künstlern und dem Publikum weltweit erlebt hatte. Die erste enthielt 29 ungewöhnliche Ereignisse. Dann ging ich eines Morgens im April 1995 in das Studio des SFB, baute meine Instrumente auf (Schlagzeug Elektronik, elektronisch verstärkte Objekte) und machte einen Soundcheck. Ich schaute auf meine Liste und wählte diese neun Geschichten aus. Dann begann ich zu spielen, zu singen und zu sprechen. Es ist eine seltsame Welt!

David Moss

D   RICHARD HUNT,
    SCOTT RAYBOULD:
    Z3 ASSOCIATES
✿   JUNGLE: THE EXTREME COLLECTION,
    VOLUME III: VARIOUS ARTISTS
●   B9 RECORDS
P   DEREK GAMBLE
■   CD COVER
✿   RIPE MASTERS VOL. 02:
    VARIOUS ARTISTS
●   RIPE RECORDINGS
P   RICHARD HUNT
■   CD COVER
✈   UK

D   DOMINIKA HASSE
D   NICOLE WISCH:
    K/PLEX
✿   MANY, MANY VOICES
    ROBERTO PACI DALÒ,
    ISABELLA BORDONI
✿   MOSS TALES:
    DAVID MOSS
●   THE LISTENING ROOM/
    EDEL COMPANY
■   INSIDE OF CD CASE
    GERMANY

so is de la soul, cursed or not?

P.S. 3

Andrew Emery
investigates

The New York Times has called them 'The thinking person's Hip-Hoppers'. Others have described them as a gang of hippies. They came out of Long Island, NY, in 1988, were managed by Lyor Cohen of Rush Management, received critical applause for their work, but few financial rewards. Bad luck appears to have dogged them from the beginning. Release after release has failed to make the impact they deserved. They cast guests on their tracks, only for those guests to disappear from the mainstream. Not only that, a key member of the crew was struck down by spinal meningitis and then suffered a nervous breakdown. Now recovered, he, like the others, has become a parent. They no longer have illusions about music-making and its makers. It's no longer

THERE'S ONLY been a select few: the ones who force the world to change gear. They pioneer new sounds and reinvent the future before it's happened. Who are they? Well, there's Bam, Flash, Eric B & Rakim, Public Enemy, KRS-1, Ultramagnetic MCs and may be Wu-Tang. De La Soul definitely. They're Posdnuos, DJ Maseo and Dave, sometimes known as Trugoy The Dove.

That's why, after sniffing the fetid halitosis of tired MCs who aspire to nothing more ambitious than a murderous, conniving life-style, the latest De La Soul album, 'Stakes Is High', comes to us like a breath of fresh air.

De La Soul isn't like a gaggle of ordinary Rappers, most of whom are the rent boys and prostitutes of the music world - even more so than pop acts.

While pop stars and chartbound teenage boy-groups are honest about their aims, many of today's B-Boys and B-Girls pretend they're producing Art for Art's sake and choosing to add to Hip-Hop culture merely to refine its texture. But, at the slightest whiff of money, they'll turn any trick. We act like we're principled, but very few of us hold to our scruples. Like the man said on 'In The Woods', 'Fuck being hard, Posdnuos is complicated'.

Say what you like, De La Soul rates highly in the honesty stakes.

Four albums deep and its members still don't want to go pop just for fame and gold. The crew has been popular and just as unpopular, but it's always chosen its own way forward. Not even the severest critic would deny De La Soul's creativity, fascination and appeal which always better than a pile of sliced records.

'Stakes...' is the sound of Soul's three members, men at the height of their powers. With guests such as Zhane, Common and Mos Def (formerly of UTD), they rock the party and still manage to remain intelligent and original.

When wack MCs hear De La Soul splashing in the deep end of the pool, may be they'll want to graduate from treading water in the shallow end of the pool and give up posturing to actually become individuals of distinctive flavor. One, two, three, 'aha a new

POSDNUOS: We never died. No, it was just us saying that death was the next plane and we were shedding an image. We're here and we consider ourselves public speakers 'cos from 'Plug Tunin'', we didn't do what the normal MC does in regular language. Public speakers means being a Supamcee for us; 'cos we just go our own way with a lot of symbolism and a lot of ciphering.

DOWNLOW: But I've heard that you intend to split after this or the next album.
DAVE:There's no splitting up for us. We've always said that if things weren't looking too bright for our careers, we'd bow out gracefully and have people remember us for what we've done. If we continue, we continue. If it ends, then let it end.

DOWNLOW: Is there a De La Soul curse? I ask because many of your guests on the different tracks have faded into obscurity. I'm talking about Don Newkirk, for instance. Shorty No Mas, Jeff from The last mack daddy on the left.
DAVE: Nah, it's not a curse. We just give everybody an opportunity to shine. Jeff, for instance, he never wanted to rhyme. He just did it 'cos we asked him. Shorty No Mas, she just got on and did her thing and then got more familiar with others in the industry and got with them. I think she's working with Beat Minerz. Don Newkirk is still around the way, producing. Everybody is successful in their own way. We even allowed the derelict on the street around the corner from our accountants.

DOWNLOW: What determined your choice of guests on this LP?
POSDNUOS: We always try to bring in new people. We just get into natural happenings. We go down with Mos Def through just knowing him. Then on '4-More', we were thinking who could be best for matching our style and that was Zhane. We always admired what Common Sense has done and then Dave ran into him a lot in the DC area and they exchanged numbers. He kept in touch and we kept him in mind.

DOWNLOW: Biz always seems to be popping up on your tracks. Why's that?
DAVE: Biz is just good people. I remember Biz when used to come to our high school and pass out flyers. From then on, we've appreciated what he's done for Hip-Hop and we've become good friends. So when he's willing to lend his unique voice and character we're always gonna invite him in to do something.

DOWNLOW: For the first time Prince Paul is absent from production duties and this seems to have made the choice of samples less eclectic, more stripped down, and there are also less skits.
POSDNUOS: We all did the production with a couple of outsiders. Spearhead X from Atlanta, O.G. down with Diggin' in the Gates crew and from Detroit, there's J.D. who's managed by Q Tip. And also Skeff Anselem. The element missing is the Zenies. That's definitely Paul. The skits were always from us, but the bugging out, the craziness, Paul brought that to us and took it to the far left. Also, with so many people coming out with skits on their albums, it made us feel like we ran too many skits after 'De La Soul Is Dead'.

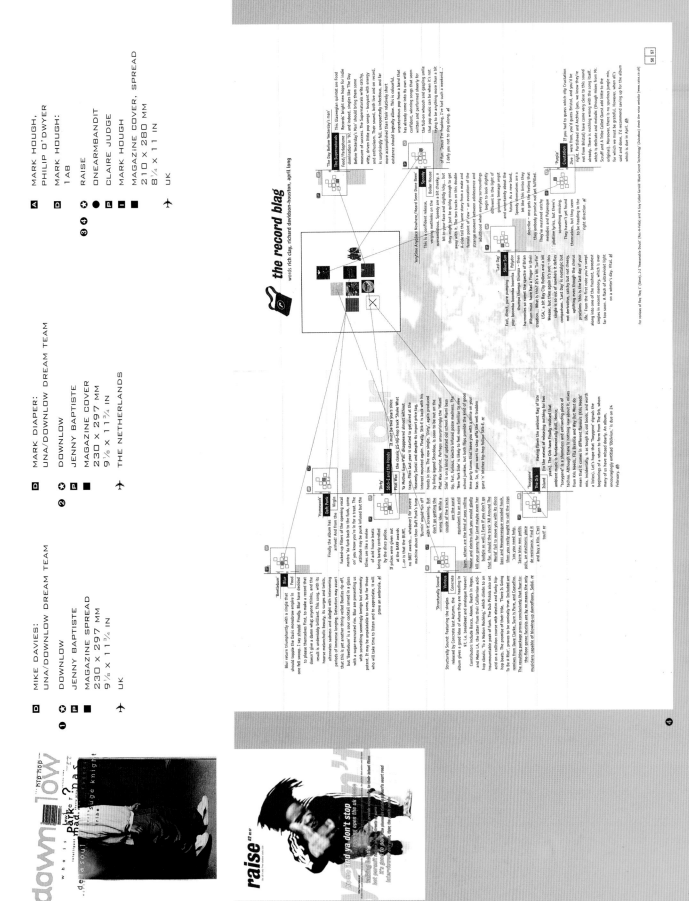

MIKE DAVIES:
UNA/DOWNLOW DREAM TEAM
DOWNLOW
JENNY BAPTISTE
MAGAZINE SPREAD
230 x 297 MM
9⅛ x 11¾ IN
UK

MARK DIAPER:
UNA/DOWNLOW DREAM TEAM
DOWNLOW
JENNY BAPTISTE
MAGAZINE COVER
230 x 297 MM
9⅛ x 11¾ IN
THE NETHERLANDS

MARK HOUGH,
PHILIP O'DWYER
MARK HOUGH:
1AB
RAISE
ONEARMBANDIT
CLAIRE JUDGE
MARK HOUGH
MAGAZINE COVER, SPREAD
210 x 280 MM
8¼ x 11 IN
UK

the record blag

words rich clay, richard davidson-houston, april long

56 57

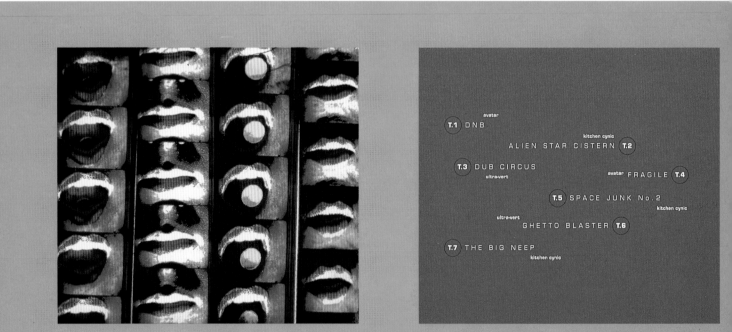

T.1 DNB
avatar

ALIEN STAR CISTERN T.2
kitchen cynic

T.3 DUB CIRCUS
ultra-vert

FRAGILE T.4
avatar

T.5 SPACE JUNK No. 2
kitchen cynic

GHETTO BLASTER T.6
ultra-vert

T.7 THE BIG NEEP
kitchen cynic

A	MARTIN FISHER	P	MIKE MILLER
D	IAN: VIVID	I	MIKE MILLER
✪	SCHTUMM BROWSER: VARIOUS ARTISTS	■	CD COVER, CONCERTINA, INSIDE OF CD CASE
●	SCHTUMM PRODUCTIONS LTD	✈	UK

■ **D** ANDREW FOSTER: ■ ORIGINAL ARTWORK FOR CD CONCERTINA
MONSTER 1510 x 315 MM
59½ x 12⅜ IN

✪ SPIRITUALISED

■ ANDREW FOSTER ✈ UK

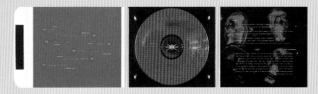

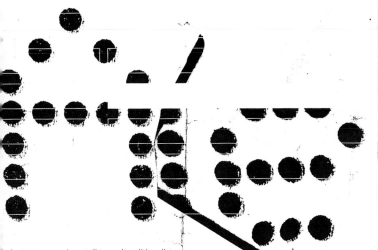

'n between experimentalists and traditionalists.

"We're interested in originality rather than extreme experimentation," explains Sean Booth in a distinctive North of England accent. Like many of their fellow electronic pioneers you'll find Autechre filed in the techno section of your local megastore, but barriers are being broken down faster than they can be rebuilt, and trying to define the Autechre sound is a tricky one. As Sean says: "We've given up." Seriously. Rob Brown, the other half comes to the rescue. "If you can find a frozen lake and throw stones across it that'd be one of our favourite tracks." Sean: "People say we've got a sound or style, but we don't necessarily think that's the case. I'm sure we probably do sound like other people to them, but to us every track is different. We listen to all sorts of shit (from hip-hop, Meat Beat Manifesto to Unsane) and you can't keep away from influences but I don't think it sounds like any particular thing. We don't think about other music when we write."

Autechre have for some years now been quietly making some of the most interesting electronic music around. I say quietly because Autechre are two fairly unassuming chaps who thankfully aren't the types to be going on stage trying to whip up an empty-headed crowd into a state of frenzy. Autechre make the listener work to get into the groove, but conversely, turn up

expecting a session of uneasy listening and you might wish you'd w your Pumas. If Autechre had their way they'd be playing "small intim venues with a good sound system but not a lot of light and no stage A fact that was borne out when I spoke to them at the somewhat misnomered Leisure Lounge in Holborn, London, where they were supposedly supporting Meat Beat Manifesto (they came on last), a doing their damndest to be allowed to play from off-stage. In the na of tradition they relented and carted their gear into the audience's f of vision for the duration of their set.

My first encounter with Autechre was supporting fellow Warp a Seefeel (Sean calls Warp "the best label in the world" and the freed

immerse

sound(e)scapes

techno
ambient
atmospherics
industrial
noise
jazz
electronica
fusion
graphics
film
print

autechre
tomato v underworld
meat beat manifesto
staalplaat
download
jenny randles

❶

❷

9 771359 782015   01   IMM 001 | £2.75

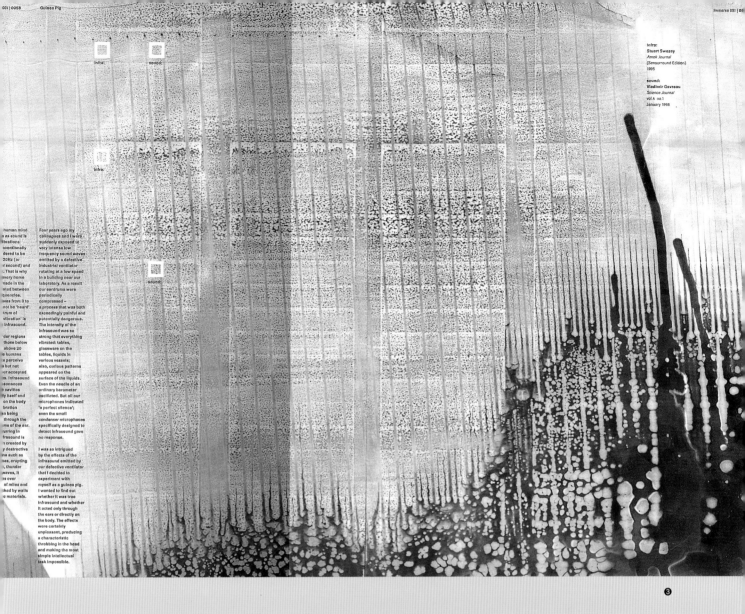

infra:
Stuart Swezey
Amok Journal
(Sensuround Edition)
1995

sound:
Vladimir Gavreau
Science Journal
vol.4 no.1
January 1968

human mind
as sound is
vibrations
conventionally
dered to be
20Hz (or
r second) and
. That is why
every home
made in the
ted between
quencies.
ves from 0 to
not be 'heard'.
trum of
vibration' is
infrasound.

der regions
those below
above 20
e humans
o perceive
s but not
er accepted
sonances
e cavities
ly itself and
on the body
bration
an being
through the
ms of the ear.
urring in
frasound is
created by
y destructive
na such as
es, erupting
, thunder
waves, it
es over
of miles and
cked by walls
c materials.

Four years ago my
colleagues and I were
suddenly exposed to
very intense low
frequency sound waves
emitted by a defective
industrial ventilator
rotating at a low speed
in a building near our
laboratory. As a result
our eardrums were
periodically
compressed –
a process that was both
exceedingly painful and
potentially dangerous.
The intensity of the
infrasound was so
strong that everything
vibrated: tables,
glassware on the
tables, liquids in
various vessels;
also, curious patterns
appeared on the
surface of the liquids.
Even the needle of an
ordinary barometer
oscillated. But all our
microphones indicated
'a perfect silence';
even the small
condenser microphones
specifically designed to
detect infrasound gave
no response.

I was so intrigued
by the effects of the
infrasound emitted by
our defective ventilator
that I decided to
experiment with
myself as a guinea pig.
I wanted to find out
whether it was true
infrasound and whether
it acted only through
the ears or directly on
the body. The effects
were certainly
unpleasant, producing
a characteristic
throbbing in the head
and making the most
simple intellectual
task impossible.

❸

A   ADAM MILLS,
    ROGER FAWCETT-TANG,
    MATHEW F. RILEY,
    TOBY MCFARLAN POND
D   ADAM MILLS,
    ROGER FAWCETT-TANG:
    LEMONADE DESIGN,
    STRUKTUR DESIGN
❶ ✪ IMMERSE 001
P   TOBY MCFARLAN POND
■   MAGAZINE COVER
    210 x 297 MM
    8 1/4 x 11 5/8 IN
✈   UK

A   ADAM MILLS,
    ROGER FAWCETT-TANG,
    MATHEW F. RILEY
D   ADAM MILLS:
    LEMONADE DESIGN
❷❸ ✪ IMMERSE 001
■   MAGAZINE SPREAD
    210 x 297 MM
    8 1/4 x 11 5/8 IN
✈   UK

❶
❸

YOU GOTTA
FIGHT
FOR YOUR RIGHT TO
PARTY

RAGE AGAINST THE WAR MACHINE: ANDREW MUELLER FRONTLINE ASSEMBLIES: MARTIN K

YOU GOTTA
FIGHT
FOR YOUR RIGHT TO
PARTY

RAGE AGAINST THE WAR MACHINE: ANDREW MUELLER
FRONTLINE ASSEMBLIES: MARTIN K

It's Babylon out there. Beyond the walled gates of Christiania, Copenhagen hums its discordant tune of business and vice. Deep-frozen Danish family life creaks and trickles along the pavements. Taxi drivers rev like Formula One psychos and the police cackle and plot. But inside the free town of Christiania, all is peace, tranquillity, dogs without strings and banana-shaped houses.

A crumbling aura of hippy idealism lingers on around this former military base, first squatted by alternative Dane droogs in the '70s. The communal council are holding a meeting. The dope dealers on Pusher Street are benignly dealing. And, into this oasis of higgledy piggledy drop-out semi-sufficiency, strides Neneh Cherry, a diva of many disguises, dropping in on one of her many passes.

"It's beautiful man," says Neneh, as we tramp over a wooden bridge, surveying the quaint wooden lakeside houses. "So weird to think it used to be a military base. The lake's probably full of mines."

Appropriately, Neneh is in army clobber today, Clumpy boots and camouflage gear. But we're not on rap-soul manoeuvres this afternoon. It is rather, another holistic day for a well-integrated life. Thus it is that Neneh Cherry is combining a media assault on the Danes with a family outing and a visit to the site of her Christiania school holidays. Never before has a singer as influential and formidable as Signora Cherry made such an organic return.

"Wow, wicked! Check out the bird, man," says Neneh's gangling half-brother Christian. "He's just cruisin' up there." And we all look up and check the seagull riding the air currents above the upper-crusty houses and concur at once that the feathered bro' is indeed cruising, and that the sight is certainly a wicked one.

Christian, a part-time teacher who lives in Copenhagen, has turned up at a house belonging to one of Neneh's "sisterwoman" friends. The house appears to have been built by the same architect who designed the one for the old woman who lived in a shoe. It is pixie-cute and lovely. The rambling garden is lovely, too, and the little posse of family and folks who've come to hang out with Neneh sit on the wooden veranda and luxuriate in the loveliness of it all. Lovely.

If you wanted to believe that Neneh was the Mum of Earth, and a lapsed flower child as well, the Hippyland pastoral tableau would provide ample evidence. But the Cherry roots are far more tangled than this. One of her other brothers, Eagle Eye, who has come down from Stockholm to hang with us, makes a wisecrack about Christian's new, fully-fluffed Afro-hair style. "I am Afro Nanny!" declares Christian, dandling Neneh's three-month-old daughter, Mabel, on his knee.

"Oh yes," says Neneh. "Just as long as I'm not Afro Mammy!"

Typecast Neneh Cherry at your peril. The life path which led her to smash through the pop codes at the end of the '80s with her rap-soul-rough grrrl 'Buffalo Stance', and which currently sees her putting out a highly emotionally-charged third album of wildly collaged soul, Man, has too many twists. As we tramp through Christiania the memories of '70s visits with her Swedish painter mother, Moki, come drifting back.

Back then it was Hell's Angels, hard drugs and disorganisation and the young Neneh was not amused. "We always thought it was really dirty and horrible," she recalls. "Get me out! I want to go and get a hot dog! And all you could get was miso soup and tahini beans!"

Nor was she particularly approving of the tuned-out drifters who used to clutter up the boho family home in south Sweden. "Nagging, yoga-ing and 'not giving anything out'."

Rebellious, hippy child? Well, not quite. "I wanted to be straight," she remembers. "I wanted a bungalow! And a Volvo. I used to get so angry with my mum because all the kids that I went to school with had mums that baked nice crusty pies, not heavy, dense wholemeal loaves. But looking at it now I can really appreciate what she gave us with all the moving and to-ing and fro-ing. And now I'm starting to do the same things myself, to the point where we're thinking now of getting a camper van so we can pack it all up and and do little funny ragga family holidays on wheels!"

You're becoming your mother.

"God. What a scary thought! No, I mean, I wish. She's quiet cool. I hope I can be like her when I'm 50."

Neneh may consider herself living in New York, designing internet web sites for adolescent girls who want to talk 'pubes, coming on bleeding blood'. Her daughter, meanwhile, at just the other side of 30, is still vigorously offering to define herself against a famously complex background.

Her biological father was a Sierra Leonean percussionist, but she was raised by Moki and modern jazz trumpet trailblazer Don Cherry. Her teenage years were split between being the only black girl in Swedish no town and apprentice B-girl life in New York. She went on the road with her dad's jazz band and lived upstairs from Talking Heads' Tina Weymouth. And at 16 she hooked up with the punky-reggae-jazz edge of Bristol and London punk in the form of The Pop Group and The Slits, eventually finding her singing voice fronting the funk-punk experimentalism of Rip Rig And Panic.

It's six years since Raw Like Sushi, the Tim Simenon-produced collaboration with her then-boyfriend [now husband] Cameron McVey [aka Booga Bear], broke all the rap rules, and four years since her last album, Homebrew, pulled itself from the pressurised aftermath of her precipitous fame. But a couple of well-earned circumstances attend her return.

One is that the live Neneh experience was underexplored first time round, whereas this time a full rock band/tourburn rubber blitz is planned. The other is that both thematically and musically, everything that she stood for back then is still way current now. You could say that while Neneh Cherry has been living out in Spain, soaking up the next set of influences, the world has been catching up.

What have you been doing, Neneh?

"I dunno. Getting laid or something. No, I don't know, what've I been doing? The usual. Having kids. Crap like that."

DENMARK

"Kootchi is about that moment when you just fancy everything about a person, and you just want to nibble at the flab hanging out the side of their T-shirt."

PASCAL BÉJEAN:
BLEU ÉLASTIQUE

L'ALLUMEUSE:
NINA MORATO

POLYDOR

ÉLODIE LACHAUD

CD PACK
155 × 235 MM
6⅛ × 9¼ IN

FRANCE

PASCAL BÉJEAN:
BLEU ÉLASTIQUE

VERTIGO!:
VARIOUS ARTISTS

VERVE

MAÏ LUCAS

INSIDE OF CD CASE

FRANCE

27

THE HIP HOP UNDERGROUND *downlow*

D MARK DIAPER,
BIRGIT EGGERS:
DOWNLOW MAGAZINE

✪ DOWNLOW – THE HIP
HOP UNDERGROUND:
VARIOUS ARTISTS

● BEECHWOOD MUSIC

P BIRGIT EGGERS

■ CD COVER,
BOOKLET

✈ THE NETHERLANDS

Extra special thanks to: My dad, for being a good mate; Mark D and all the downlow's crazy designers for putting up with my bullshit; Fusion at Echoes, Pebo & MK at Deal Real (it's still Handspun to me) for hooking me up; Big Agent Moulder (The Star Wars freak!) Tim, John, Kate & all at Beechwood (Easy!); Brendan (oui, oui, oui), my brother, my ace, Wayne Clarke (for all the classic kidz), Izzy sessions in the nine p(zzy!); Diggy O. Mr Trevor Jackson (without you man the downlow would probably be dead. Thanks so much!); Kemi (thanks for comin' up with the business); downlow Entertainment, Fondle 'Em, Echo, Sound Of Money, Word Sound, Raw Shack, Correct & Knowledge of Self records. To them and everybody trying to make it happen for themselves, independently, this album is dedicated. Plus everyone who has contributed to the downlow, talked to me and realised I'm not human...Thanks for buying, reading and listening to this album. You've made me a happy alien from Pornos 5 - Mat ©

1.INTRO - *Die young* Produced by Kemi for Patch Face Productions. Licensed courtesy of Tea Boy Music.
2.GODFATHER DON *I was forgotten* (R.Chapman for dontown music BMI) Produced by Godfather Don Copyright Control.
Licensed courtesy of Fondle 'em Recordings. 3.FRANKENSTEIN *Frankensteins pain* (Frankenstein). Published & administered by
society of composers/music publishers of Canada (socan)/ knowledge of self, licensed courtesy of Knowledge Of Self. 4.AL TARIQ
Do yo thang (Al Tariq) Produced by the Beatnuts, Published by Bleu Nyte Music (ASCAP)/Inkyju (ASCAP)/Mathematics Publishing
(ASCAP) Licensed courtesy of Grindstone Entertainment. 5.ROOTS MANUVA *Next type of motion* (R.Smith) Mixed by Jam Ei,
Produced by Roots Manuva Simit, Copyright control, Licensed courtesy of Sound of Money Records. 6.CHILL ROB G *Let me
know something* (R.Frasier/N.Bell) Produced by Disc-tinct Echo Music. Licensed courtesy
of Echo International (U.S.A.) 7.LEWIS PARKER *Mysteries of life* (L.Parker/A.Dublin/DJ Bias) Copyright control. Licensed courtesy
of Bite It! Recordings Ltd. 8.EAST FLAT BUSH PROJECT *Tried by 12* (R.Smith/S.Bellamy) Produced by S. Bellamy, Published
by Haripa Music, Licensed courtesy of Kickin Records Ltd. 9.BLAK TWANG *Real estate* (T.Olabode/C.Matthias) Produced by
DJ Rumple/Taipanic published by Warner Chappell/Copyright control. Licensed courtesy of Sound of Money 10.J-LIVE *Braggin
writes* (J.Cadet/G.Sulmers) Produced by Georges Sulmers. Published by only Child's Brother's Music/Havick Music. Licensed courtesy
of Raw Shack Music. 11.PRINCE PAUL *You made me* (P.Paul) Produced by Prince Paul. Published by Prinse Pawl Musick/BMI.
Licensed courtesy of Word Sound Recordings. 12.OUTRO - *TCB* Produced by Kemi for Patch Face Productions. Licensed courtesy of
Tea Boy Music.

downlow

THE HIP HOP UNDERGROUND streetsounds

SOUND010

```
0 16553 35102 0
```

1.INTRO die young
2.GODFATHER DON i was forgotten
3.FRANKENSTEIN frankenstein's pain
4.AL TARIQ do yo' thang
5.ROOTS MANUVA next type of motion
6.CHILL ROB G let me know something
7.LEWIS PARKER mysteries of life
8.EAST FLAT BUSH PROJECT tried by 12
9.BLAK TWANG real estate
10.J-LIVE braggin writes
11.PRINCE PAUL you made me
12.OUTRO tcb

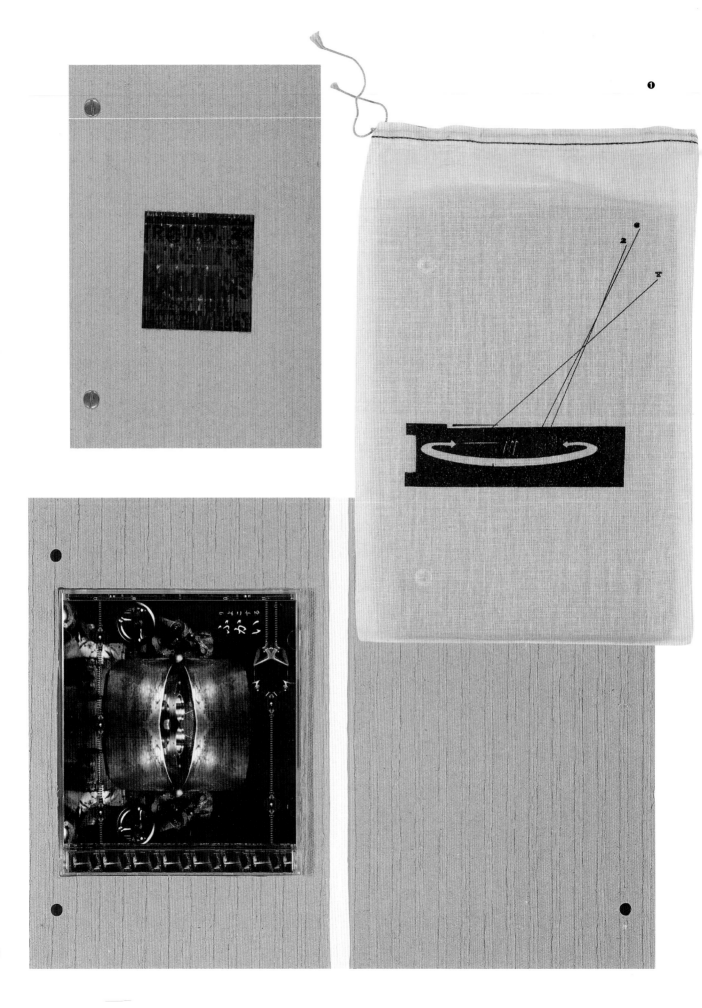

RENT book, music and lyrics by

JONATHAN LARSON

NEDERLANDER THEATRE, NYC

directed by **MICHAEL GREIF**

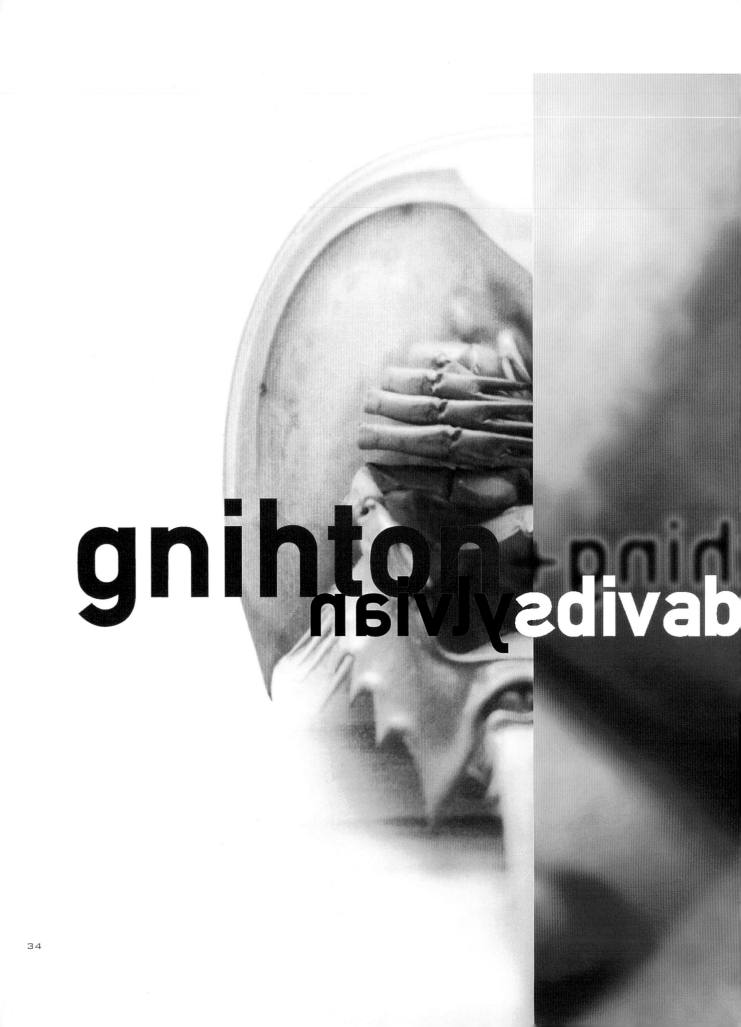

nothing

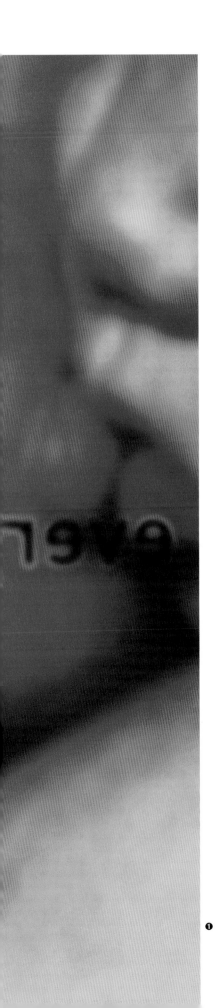

②

❶

Power

CLASSIC *f*M 100-102

A	BRIAN CONNOLLY: BST. BDDP	P	NADAV KANDER
❶ ✪	POWER:	■	96 SHEET POSTER
❷ ✪	EXHILARATION: CLASSIC FM		12.2 x 3 M 40 x 10 FT
●	CLASSIC FM	✈	UK

EXHILARATION

CLASSIC ƒM 100·102

mikhail

pletnev haydn

piano sonatas
c minor • e flat minor • c major

variations in f minor

7243 5 45254 2 1

❶

7243 5 45130 2 2

piano concertos klavierkonzerte **9 & 20**

mozart

pletnev

deutsche kammerphilharmonie

❷

A JEREMY HALL

D CORNELIA REINARD,
RACHAEL DINNIS:
LIPPA PEARCE

❶ ✪ HAYDN — PIANO SONATAS:
MIKHAIL PLETNEV

D RACHAEL DINNIS:
LIPPA PEARCE

❷ ✪ MOZART, PIANO CONCERTOS
9 & 20: MIKHAIL PLETNEV,
DEUTSCHE KAMMERPHILHARMONIE

● VIRGIN CLASSICS

℗ ROBERT BARBER

■ CD COVER

✈ UK

Concerto pour piano · Concert champêtre · Concerto pour orgue

City of London Sinfonia

Jean-Bernard Pommier · Maggie Cole · Gillian Weir · **Richard Hickox**

➊

Concerto pour deux pianos · Sinfonietta · Aubade

City of London Sinfonia

Jean-Bernard Pommier · Anne Queffélec · **Richard Hickox**

➋

A JEREMY HALL
D RACHAEL DINNIS:
LIPPA PEARCE
➊ ✪ POULENC – PIANO AND ORGAN
CONCERTOS:
➋ ✪ POULENC – SINFONIETTA:
RICHARD HICKOX,
CITY OF LONDON SINFONIA

● VIRGIN CLASSICS
■ ALI CAMPBELL
■ CD COVER
✈ UK

❶

❷

1

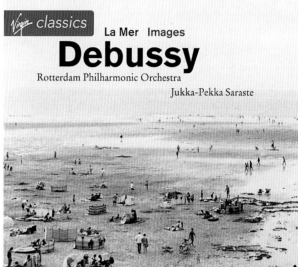

2

3

4

ARTICLE 11. (EARLY DEPARTURE.

ear Humpfrey Valentine,
............thought it best to drop a
ine today. A foreign tongue has moved my way but she´es to quick
o lay at length beside me. I said, "come to me" To much I can´t
isclose, "come for me" Above the thought of her arriving looms
he well in which I´m sliding into her. Suddenly ! she finds
erself light a cigarette before I come myself then it all goes
uiet. Mr Humpfrey Valentine this foreign tongue has served
e a complex. Her stainless reputation has been shot with her
emptation of departure. I´d rise in a moment of corse if she´d
ffer me a taste of reward

    Am I just insatiable.

    Yours Sincerely

    Mr H. P. Whiteson.

    P.S. Would she hurt me, Could she take me,
    Will she hate herself for it.....

P.B. JNR.
NIKOLAJ BLOCH
TOMMAS ALEXANDER ARNBY
SIR GEORGE

SUBCIRCUS WOULD LIKE TO
THANK EVERYONE WHO INSPIRED AND
CONTRIBUTED TO OUR FIRST ALBUM.

They found him
crashing waves
against static
fields. They pull
his hands out of
the sky Comics.
Dirty make up your
FIX when crystal
forms your circus
bones merging with
the ambulance.
In a box behind the
carnival, U taste
delicious when your
dry Comica Muh Im
sure his body
forms but he´es to
quick to kiss the
naked lunatic.. I
FALL TO SLEEP WE
CAN´T
RESIST. I FALL
TO SLEEP
WE CAN´T #5

❶

❷

0630-13316-2

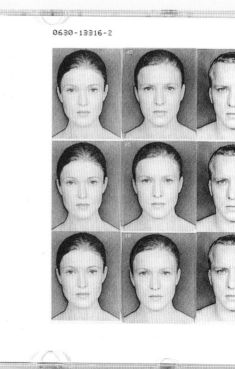

CAROUSEL

SUBCIRCUS

THE BELOVED
X

- ▣ ROB CRANE,
  BRIGITTE COGGON:
  SATELLITE
- ❶ ✪ CAROUSEL:
  SUBCIRCUS
- ● ECHO
- ▣ MARIA MOCHNACZ
- ■ CD CONCERTINA
- ✈ UK

- ▣ STEPHANIE NASH,
  ANTHONY MICHAEL:
  MICHAEL NASH ASSOCIATES
- ❷ ✪ X:
  THE BELOVED
- ● EASTWEST
- ▣ JULIAN BROAD
- ■ INSIDE OF CD CASE
- ✈ UK

underworld : second toughest in the infants

Ceramic-cow

you look like a rat amazing stinky!

smell squatting altered by this bott
chemical hunting interests at the b
alley lieing in thier fever beds
and conversations with respects sw
wating for cabs a phone box a ligh
your answerphone i left my voice
the machine with nothing in return
pre-recorded humour restricted se
love you

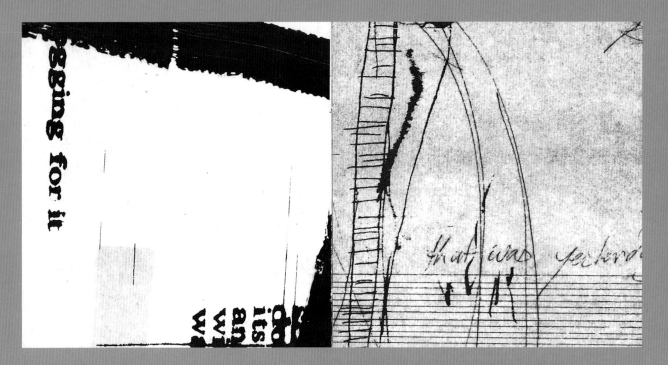

gging for it

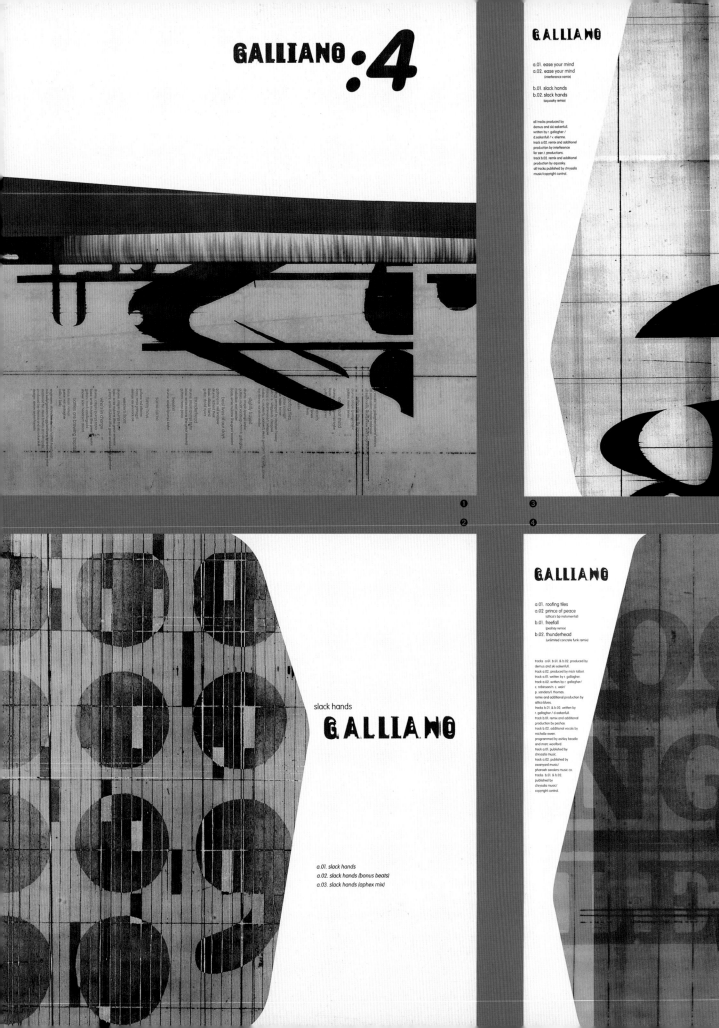

GALLIANO :4

① ②   ③ ④

slack hands
GALLIANO

a.01. slack hands
a.02. slack hands (bonus beats)
a.03. slack hands (aphex mix)

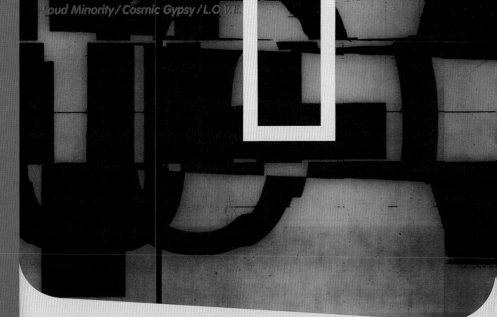

⑤
⑥

United Future Organization *Loud Minority*

CANAL CAN'T STAY STILL TONIGHT
MUST HAVE SOME NEWS TO TELL
A BOY WAS PUSHED IN THIS AFTERNOON
ALTHOUGH HE'S CLAIMING NOW THAT HE FELL

I SIT HERE AND I WONDER
AS I ALWAYS THINK TOO MUCH
IF I COULD SLOW MY MIND DOWN A WHILE
EVERYTHING'S IN A RUSH

THEN THE MOON STARTS PUSHING UP
DROPPING BITS DOWN ON US
STARS TRY TO STEAL THE NIGHT
BUT IT'S ALREADY FULL OF WINKS AND FIGHT
LOCAL TURNS BOUND FOR CARLISLE
WITH A THOUSAND ROOFING TILES
MOON STARTS DROPPING ALL AROUND
YOUR VOICE MAKES THE ONLY SOUND

RICH MAN FOR AN HOUR OR MORE
CAN BE A LITTLE DIRTY TO TELL
AND MY FRIEND'S MUM GOES WALKING BY
SAYS SHE'S KIND OF TIRED BUT SHE'S WELL

AND I SIT HERE AND I WONDER
BOTH A BLESSING AND A CURSE
NOTHING TIME MIGHT HAVE GOT BETTER
CAN'T STOP TILL I'VE SEEN THE ONE THAT GOT

THEN THE MOON STARTS PUSHING UP
DROPPING BITS DOWN ON US
STARS TRY TO STEAL THE NIGHT
BUT IT'S ALREADY FULL OF WINKS AND FIGHT
LOCAL TURNS BOUND FOR CARLISLE
WITH A THOUSAND ROOFING TILES
MOON STARTS DROPPING ALL AROUND
YOUR VOICE MAKES THE ONLY SOUND
THIS SONG YOU WERE RIGHT
THERE'S A STRAY DOG HERE
I BET HE WON'T BITE
PAST GRAFFITI BY THE BRIDGE
TWO SHOPPING TROLLEYS HALF A FRIDGE
UP THE STEPS THAT TAKE YOU TO THE ROAD
CRACKED ROOFING TILES HE SPLIT THE LOAD
MOON HEART DROPPING ALL AROUND
YOUR VOICE MAKE THE ONLY SOUND

u nd erw

: born slippy .NUXX ; b

a side; born slippy/NUXX.
MIX. written/produced/mi
own, 1996. junior recordin
0181 960 4495, facsimile 01
management: jukes produ
by rtm/disc. made in engl

for more information send a SAE [or IR

jbo44   JUN

5 026734 004461 >

rld : born slippy .

lippy :NUXX ,DARREN PRICE REMIX ban style. [ALEX REECE MIX]

; born slippy/NUXX. DARREN PRICE MIX, banstyle/ALEX REECE
y UNDERWORLD [smith/hyde/emerson]. ℗ + © junior boys
, the saga centre, 326 kensal road, london w10 5bz, telephone
60 3256. published by underworld/sherlock holmes music.
, telephone 0171 286 9532. manufactured and distributed

uk] to: UNDERWORLD, c/o UV, 20 church street, isleworth, middlesex, tv7 6dp, uk.

taken from the film
'trainspotting'
plus alex reece remix

A CHRIS PRIEST

D ANDY ALTMANN, DAVID ELLIS, CHRIS PRIEST; WHY NOT ASSOCIATES

1 ✱ I NEED ANOTHER:

✱ DODGY

● A&M RECORDS

P JULIAN GERMANE

■■ RECORD SLEEVE

305 x 305 MM

12 x 12 IN

✈ UK

A STEPHAN LAUHOFF

D ANDREAS LAUHOFF; 3 DE LUXE

2 ● RAVE CITY 4

● RAVE CITY GMBH

I NICK SCHWEIGER

■■ BOOKLET

210 x 150 MM

8¼ x 5⅝ IN

✈ GERMANY

DODGY SAY: LET'S CUT SOME RUG KIDDIES

GNOMES, L 2 R: MICKEY, NIGEL, MATHEW, ANDY, ANDY

"i need another" E.P.

dodgy

(the correct way to pronounce 'DODGY' is to say: 'd a a r JEE', as in darjeeling tea.)

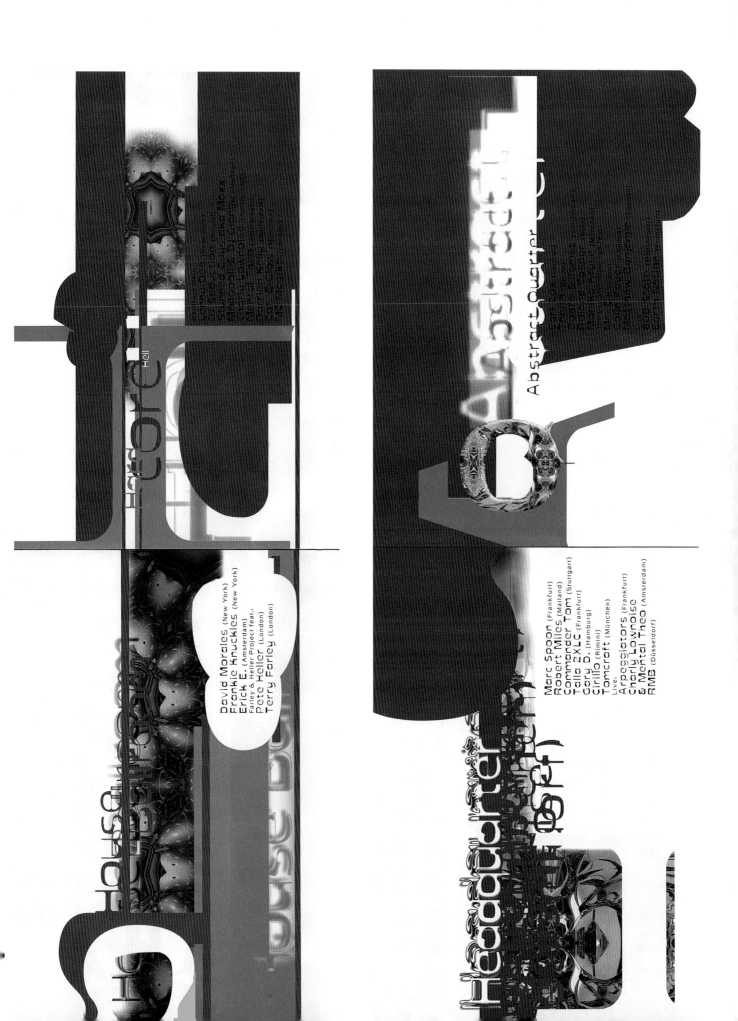

cat no. 581 624 - 7 · poly 102 / lct 0485

№ 03326

A. IN A ROOM (full version)
produced and mixed by HUGH JONES

B. OUT CLUBBING
another BOSTIN DODGY PRODUCTION
mixed from DODGY live
by JEROME DI PIETRO and PHIL MOSSMAN

all songs written and performed by
NIGEL CLARK, MATHEW PRIEST and ANDY MILLER
published by THE BERTELSMANN MUSIC GROUP

additional musicians. RICHARD PAYNE plays keyboards on all songs.
THE KICK HORNS play on *IN A ROOM*
you've heard us
now let us hear from you.
write to dodgy c/o po box 2428, london n16 8nl

pictures. DERRICK SANTINI
graphics. CHRIS PRIEST (studio barbara)
interiors. BRUNO SANTINI
on the case. JEZ PEARCE

mighty · dodgy · vibe
the way of dodgy no. 14: MAY THE ROOF OF YOUR HOUSE
NEVER FALL IN AND THOSE WITHIN, NEVER FALL OUT

DODGY · in a room

A&M Records

A CHRIS PRIEST,
JEZ PEARCE

D CHRIS PRIEST:
STUDIO BARBARA©

✪ IN A ROOM:
DODGY

● A&M RECORDS

P DERRICK SANTINI

■ RECORD SLEEVE
178 x 178 MM
7 x 7 IN

✈ UK

52

A   CHRIS PRIEST,
JEZ PEARCE

D   CHRIS PRIEST:
STUDIO BARBARA©

✪   GOOD ENOUGH:
DODGY

●   A&M RECORDS

P   DERRICK SANTINI

■   RECORD SLEEVE
178 x 178 MM
7 x 7 IN

✈   UK

53

D BRIAN WILLIAMS:
DYNAMO

✪ SILVER WRISTS:
NAIMEE COLEMAN

● EMI IRELAND

P MARC O'SULLIVAN/PHOTODISC

■ CD COVER,
INSIDE OF CD CASE

✈ IRELAND

Naimee Coleman
RUTHLESS
AFFECTION

1. RUTHLESS AFFECTION
2. SEE WHAT I SEE 3. SPECIAL

Track 1
Produced by Peter Van Hooke
Engineered by Simon Smart
Recorded at Red house Studios
Mixed at Abbey Road Studios
Track 2 & 3
Recorded upstairs at Dave's

Design and treatments at Dynamo
Original photo [Naimee] by Marc O'Sullivan

All songs composed by Naimee Coleman
Published by Copyright Control
℗ & © 1996 The copyright in this sound
recording is owned by EMI Records Ireland.

❶

"care about you"
Naimee Coleman

"care about you,"
Naimee Coleman

1.Care About You
Produced and engineered by Chris Porter
Recorded at Porterhouse Studios

2.Remind Me
Produced by Peter Van Hooke
Engineered by Simon Smart
Recorded at Red house Studios
Mixed at Abbey Road Studios

3.Care About You (Instrumental)
Produced and engineered by Chris Porter
Recorded at Porterhouse Studios

taken from the album Silver Wrists

Design and treatments at **Dynamo** / Original photo [Naimee] by **Marc O'Sullivan** / All songs composed by **Naimee Coleman**
except track 2 written by **Derek Duggan** & **Naimee Coleman** / Published by Copyright Control / ℗ & © EMI Records Ireland 1996

❷

	BRIAN WILLIAMS: DYNAMO
❶ ✪	RUTHLESS AFFECTION:
❷ ✪	CARE ABOUT YOU: NAIMEE COLEMAN
●	EMI IRELAND
℗	MARC O'SULLIVAN
■	CD COVER, CD
✈	IRELAND

PRIMAL
SCREAM

"How the fuck can you write about life in Britain today and not write about E?" Since *Trainspotting* became a film and phenomenon, Irvine Welsh has shot from cult status to fully fledged celebrity. With his new novel *Ecstasy*, which switches focus from heroin's cultural margins to the clubbing mainstream, this chemical chronicler could now become public enemy number one

Havin' it with Irvine Welsh. A few months ago, Irvine and two of his mates got hold of "the nicest E's that had been going round town for a while". It was a sunny day so they mixed up a tape of music, made three copies, placed each one in a Walkman and went outside. "We synchronised everything, the pills are fucking well in, we're coming up at the same time, hearing the same music and we're walking through town, watching football, sitting in the pub, bottles of water all round, and we got into a strange telepathy. You don't want to turn the music down so you're shouting to make yourself heard and eventually you stop speech, it's all gestures, non-verbal communications. And it does stuff, you're in this strange world and totally fucking interacting with it. It's like cyberspace. If you try taking the headphones off it's like you're falling from a great height, you can feel yourself physically fall right back down to Earth. Bang!"

Ever since his first book, *Trainspotting*, was published in 1993, Irvine Welsh has found his own uniquely cool place in the modern world. Creating a track usually seems the best way to respond to full immersion in the 'avin it, beat-driven present that Irvine inhabits. But *Trainspotting* and the books that followed it, *The Acid House* and *Marabou Stork Nightmares*, seemed as natural a response to the here and now as breakbeats and babes. And ever since *Trainspotting* became a film and phenomenon, Irvine has shot from radical cult status towards higher and higher plains of celebrity. He's even made that record, a piss-take football tune for the European Nations Cup with Primal Scream and Adrian Sherwood. "It's a really weird time for me. The whole thing about becoming successful ▶

interview by tony marcus photography by donald christie

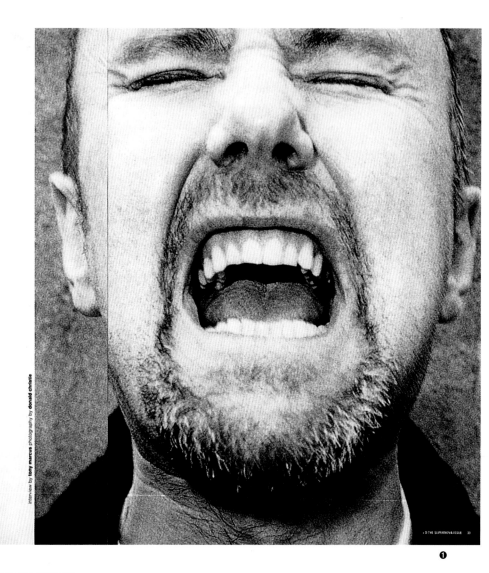

❶

❷

Ⓐ	SCOTT KING, TERRY JONES
Ⓓ	SCOTT KING, BRENDAN PARKER
✪	I-D
❶ Ⓟ	DONALD CHRISTIE
❷ Ⓟ	CRAIG MCDEAN
■	MAGAZINE COVER, SPREAD 230 x 288 MM 9 x 11⅜ IN
✈	UK

interview by **dave simpson**
photography by **kent baker**

Dismissed as Madchester's also-rans, The Charlatans gave out but never gave up. While their peers crashed and burned, Burgess and his boys simply survived. A nervous breakdown and jail sentence later, the latecomers to the party are left clutching the champagne. But is there still a price to be paid?

UP FOR IT?

When Tim Burgess was a teenager, he used to take loads of speed and run up to the top of the highest hill he could find. Nine years later he still hasn't come down. This has been the most successful year ever for The Charlatans. They've had a number one album (repeating the example of their 1990 debut, *Some Friendly*), three hit singles, numerous triumphant festival appearances and they're about to embark on their biggest UK tour to date. It's all the more surprising because none of this was meant to happen.

When they first emerged in 1989, Burgess' (some said appropriately named) Charlatans were thought of as the also-rans of baggy; Johnny-come-latelies behind the then 'Holy Triumvirate' of The Stone Roses, Happy Mondays and Inspiral Carpets. But although they may have gatecrashed the party, The Charlatans took over the decks and cranked up their own tunes. Manager Steve Harrison was opportunistic in printing up leaflets touting Burgess' boys as "the Stone Roses favourite support band" and playing on the connection. But the late '89/'90 Madchester explosion provided a springboard with which to launch The Charlatans' own narcotic concoction of existential vocals, pulverising Hammond organs and hallucinogenic, blissed-out grooves. They sold out venues before releasing a record, and their second single, *The Only One I Know*, quickly became a massive hit and one of the defining ►

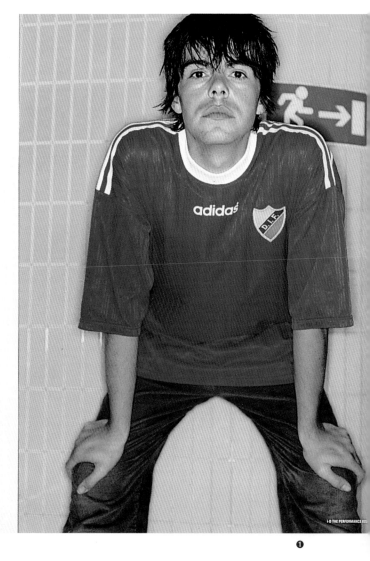

❶

❷

Ⓐ		SCOTT KING, TERRY JONES
Ⓓ		SCOTT KING, BRENDAN PARKER
✪		I-D
❶	Ⓟ	KENT BAKER
❷	Ⓟ	CRAIG MCDEAN
■		MAGAZINE COVER, SPREAD 230 x 288 MM 9 x 11⅜ IN
✈		UK

EBERHARD BLUM
BLUM
RECORDINGS
ON CD
1990-1996

An area the size of the Ryoan-ji temple garden, Kyoto, marked out in the exhibition hall of the Akademie der Künste, Berlin, served as performance and recording space for John Cage's Ryoanji in June 1995.

unterschiedlicher Härtegrade der Bleistifte wurde durch Zufallsoperationen bestimmt. Gleichzeitig fing Cage an, über ein musikalisches Werk mit dem Titel Ryoanji nachzudenken. Er entwarf eine Anzahl rechteckiger Flächen und zeichnete Teile des Umrisse der gleichen Steine, die er für seine bildnerischen Arbeiten verwendete, in diese Flächen. Die einzelnen Flächen, mit einem mikrotonalen Tonhöhenraster versehen, bilden zusammen einen ‚Garten der Klänge'. So entstanden nach und nach Partien für Flöte, Oboe, Posaune, Kontrabaß und Gesang. Die Partien können, nach einem zu erarbeitenden Zeitplan, einzeln oder in jeder beliebigen Kombination aufgeführt werden.

Zusätzlich komponierte Cage einen obligaten Schlagzeugpart. Dieser bildet – ‚leise, aber nicht im Hintergrund' – gewissermaßen die Folie des ‚weißen, geharkten Sandes' im ‚Garten der Klänge'. Der Part besteht aus einer Anzahl nicht spezifizierter Klänge, unisono gespielt, die in unregelmäßigen Abständen erklingen. Cage wollte verhindern, daß ein rhythmisches Muster zu erkennen ist. Die Gesangspartie und die Instrumentalpartien bestehen fast ausschließlich aus ‚Glissandi'. Diese sind, nach Cages Anweisungen, ‚geschmeidig zu spielen und soweit irgend möglich eher wie Klangereignisse in der Natur als wie Klänge in der Musik'. Die äußerst sparsame und stille Musik folgt dem meditativen Charakter des japanischen Gartens.

Zwei Aufführungen des Werkes fanden am 23. und 24. Juni 1995 auf Einladung der Abteilung Darstellende Kunst der Akademie der Künste Berlin innerhalb der von Dirk Scheper geleiteten Gastspielreihe PANTOMIME – MUSIK – TANZ – THEATER '95 in der großen Ausstellungshalle der Akademie statt. Eine Fläche, die der des Ryoan-ji-Steingartens entspricht, wurde mit weißen am Boden verlaufenden Leisten eingerahmt.

26

JOHN CAGE
RYOANJI
ROBERT BLACK
EBERHARD BLUM
IVEN HAUSSMANN
GUDRUN RESCHKE
JOHN PATRICK THOMAS
JAN WILLIAMS

JOHN CAGE: RYOANJI
Robert Black (contrabass), Eberhard Blum (flute), Iven Hausmann (trombone),
Gudrun Reschke (oboe), John Patrick Thomas (voice), Jan Williams (percussion)
Co-Production: Sender Freies Berlin/Akademie der Künste/hat Hut Records Ltd.
Digital recording: 22 June 1995, Akademie der Künste, Berlin.
Recording supervisor: Wolfgang Hoff, Sound engineer: Wolfgang Zülch.
Mix and CD-master by Peter Pfister,
Liner notes by Eberhard Blum, Art Lange, Yumiko Urae, and Jean Verneil,
Produced by Martin Demmler/Dirk Scheper/Pia & Werner X. Uehlinger
hatART CD 6183

Innerhalb dieser Fläche wurden fünf Spielorte, der Anordnung der Steingruppen des Gartens folgend, für die Musiker festgelegt. Für das obligate Schlagzeug, die alles verbindende Partie, wurde ein sechster Spielort innerhalb der Fläche bestimmt. Die gesamte Fläche wurde mit Sitzbänken für das hörende Publikum umstellt. Die Architektur des 1960 von Werner Düttmann entworfenen Raumes, die von weitem in den Raum dringenden Naturklänge des die Akademie umgebenden Tiergartens und die gedämpft hörbaren Klänge der Stadt bildeten einen idealen Aufführungsort für das Werk.

Der Tonmeister Wolfgang Hoff und der Toningenieur Wolfgang Zülch vom Sender Freies Berlin plazierten fünf Lautsprecher innerhalb der Fläche und ordneten sie jeweils einem Musiker zu. Die notwendigen Zuspielbänder für die fünf Partien wurden im Aufführungsraum an zwei aufeinanderfolgenden Tagen zugenommen. In den dann folgenden Proben wurden die Klänge so balanciert, daß man als Hörer zwischen den aus Lautsprechern und den im Raum erzeugten Klängen nicht unterscheiden konnte. Dieses akustische Gesamtergebnis, der ‚Garten der Klänge', wurde am 22. Juni 1995, dem Tag vor unserer ersten Aufführung, für diese CD dokumentiert. Die Gesamtdauer der Aufführung – vom Komponisten nicht vorgeschrieben – hatte ich auf eine Stunde festgelegt. Das Werk beginnt und endet immer – vom Komponisten vorgeschrieben – mit dem Schlagzeug. Die zeitliche Plazierung der anderen Partien – vom Komponisten nicht vorgeschrieben – innerhalb dieser Stunde habe ich ebenfalls im voraus bestimmt.

So ist jede Aufführung und jede Dokumentation des Werkes auf Tonträger eine ‚Photographie' der vom Komponisten vorgegebenen ‚mobilen' Bedingungen.

27

The advertising column of the Literaturhaus Berlin, announcing the CHOICE & CHANCE series in February 1993. (Typography by Ann Holyoke Lehmann.)

57

KURT SCHWITTERS
URSONATE
EBERHARD BLUM
VOICE

KURT SCHWITTERS: URSONATE
Eberhard Blum (voice)
Kurt Schwitters: Ursonate, The real dreads of the nightmare,
Ribble Bobble Pimlico, Ri Ribble
Digital recording: 29 December 1991, Studio 2/Radio DRS, Zürich,
Recording and CD-master by Peter Pfister, Produced by Pia & Werner X. Uehlinger
hatART CD 6109

Zur Ursonate

Das aus dem Jahre 1918 stammende phonetische Gedicht von Raoul Hausmann mit der Anfangszeile ‚fmsbwtözäu' war Keimzelle der Sonate in Urlaute von Kurt Schwitters. Ausgehend von diesem Material kombinierte er Vokale und Konsonanten zu Motiven, Themen und Nebenthemen, rhythmischen Elementen und Variationen, aus denen er eine musikalische Sprache schuf. So entstand in den Jahren 1921-32, immer wieder verändert und weiterausgearbeitet, die Ursonate, eine im wesentlichen klassische Sonate – die weder durch Sinn entstellt, noch von Schwitters nicht gewollter Bedeutung belastet werden sollte – mit einem ausführlichen ersten Satz, einem langsamen Teil, einem Scherzo mit Trio und einem virtuosen Finale mit Kadenz.

Schwitters hat der definitiven Fassung der Sonate, die er 1932 in seiner Zeitschrift Merz 24 veröffentlichte, einen Text mit Erläuterungen zu ihrer musikalischen Konstruktion sowie zur Ausführung und zur Aussprache der Laute vorangestellt. Der vom Schweizer Typographen Jan Tschichold im Auftrage von Schwitters entworfene graphische Gestaltung – Schwitters nannte sie das ‚Schriftsatz' – gibt zusätzlich Aufschluß über die Struktur des Werkes.

Ich habe die Ursonate zum ersten Mal im Januar 1975 aufgeführt. Das Konzert fand in New York in der Radiostation WBAI als Gastveranstaltung des Center of the Creative and Performing Arts, Buffalo, statt. In den vergangenen 21 Jahren habe ich über einhundert Aufführungen des Werkes gemacht, vom Nachtkonzert im Palastgarten in Chiraz, Perußen, bis zum Polyphonix-Festival im Museum of Modern Art, New York, und zu Ehren des verstorbenen Max Bill im Schauspielhaus Zürich.

Die folgenden SECHS SEITEN habe ich für den Kurt Schwitters Almanach 1987 (Hannover), eine Hommage zum einhundertsten Geburtstag des Künstlers, gezeichnet.

57

❶

GALINA
USTVOLSKAYA
3
MARIANNE
SCHROEDER
PIANO
SONATAS
1-6

❷

STEFAN
WOLPE
PASSACAGLIA
FIRST
RECORDINGS
1954

❸
CHRISTIAN
WOLFF
EXERCISES
EBERHARD BLUM
ROLAND DAHINDEN
STEFFEN
SCHLEIERMACHER
JAN WILLIAMS

❹
EARLE
BROWN
SYNERGY
ENSEMBLE
AVANTGARDE
LEIPZIG
CONDUCTED BY
EARLE BROWN

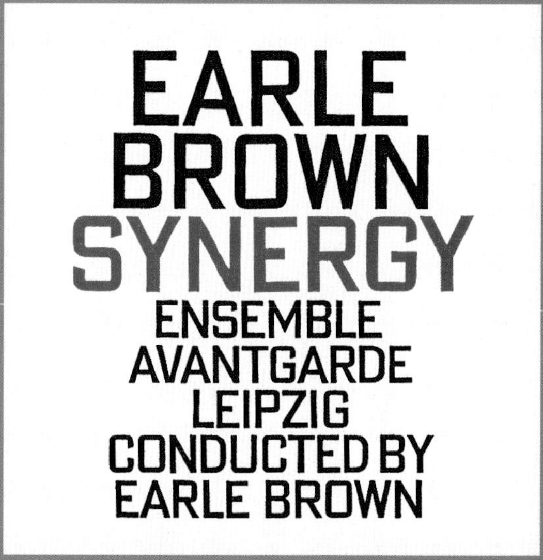

PREVIOUS SPREAD

�D   ANN HOLYOKE LEHMANN

✿   EBERHARD BLUM: RECORDINGS
     ON CD 1990–1996

●   HAT HUT RECORDS LTD

🅿   ANN HOLYOKE LEHMANN

■   CATALOGUE COVER,
     SPREADS
     280 X 210 MM
     11 X 8¼ IN

✈   GERMANY

❺

JOHN CAGE
IMAGINARY
LANDSCAPES
PERCUSSION
ENSEMBLE
DIRECTED BY
JAN WILLIAMS

❻

ALEA
ROMAN
HAUBENSTOCK-RAMATI
LUIS DE PABLO
TONA SCHERCHEN
BERND ALOIS
ZIMMERMANN
EBERHARD BLUM
FLUTE

❼

龍安寺
JOHN CAGE
RYOANJI
ROBERT BLACK
EBERHARD BLUM
IVEN HAUSMANN
GUDRUN RESCHKE
JOHN PATRICK THOMAS
JAN WILLIAMS

❽

ERNSTALBRECHT
STIEBLER
THREE IN ONE
EBERHARD BLUM
BASS FLUTE
MARIANNE SCHROEDER
PIANO
ROBYN SCHULKOWSKY
PERCUSSION
FRANCES-MARIE UITTI
VIOLONCELLO

❶–❽ ▭ ANN HOLYOKE LEHMANN
● HAT HUT RECORDS LTD
■ CD COVER
❾ ■ SLIPCASE COVER FOR 4-CD SET
✈ SWITZERLAND

❾

**ANTHONY
BRAXTON**
PIANO MUSIC
(NOTATED)
1968-1988
HILDEGARD KLEEB
PIANO

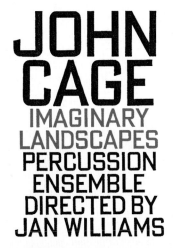

▣ KATHARINA SIEVERDING

✪ TOLLMANNHILDENBEUTEL:
    GOTTFRIED TOLLMANN AND
    RALF HILDENBEUTEL

● RECYCLE OR DIE

▣ KATHARINA SIEVERDING

▪ KATHARINA SIEVERDING

■ CD TIN COVER,
    CD IN TIN CASE
    142 X 125 MM
    5⅝ X 4⅞ IN

✈ GERMANY

◨ GOTTFRIED TOLLMANN
✪ FEARLESS:
  SOLITAIRE
● RECYCLE OR DIE
◧ GOTTFRIED TOLLMANN
■ CD TIN COVER,
  CD IN TIN CASE
  142 × 125 MM
  $5\frac{5}{8}$ × $4\frac{7}{8}$ IN
✈ GERMANY

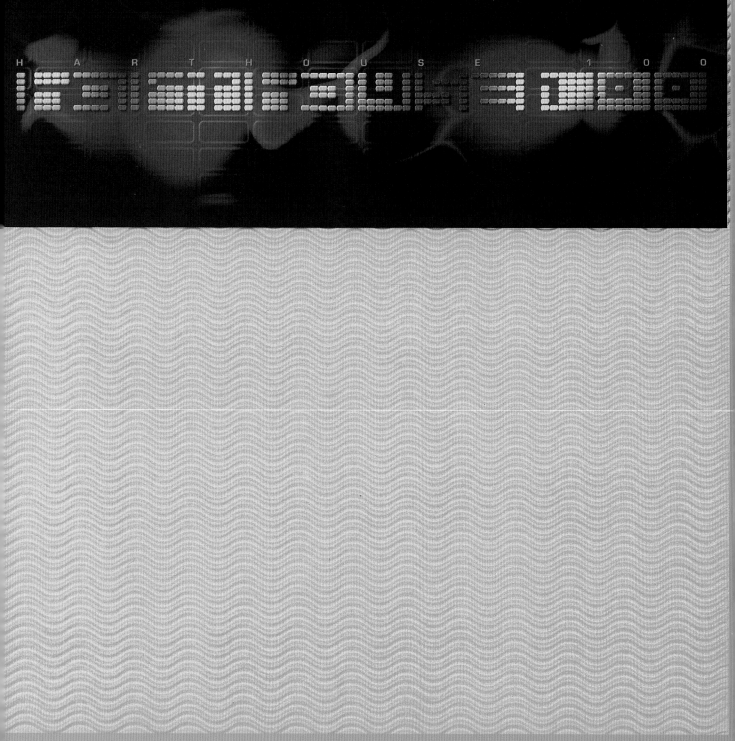

D   GEORGE DARE:
     DARE ART

✪   HARTHOUSE 100:
     VARIOUS ARTISTS

●   HARTHOUSE RECORDS

▯   GEORGE DARE

■   ALBUM SLEEVE

  ✈   GERMANY

HOME RUN

1. PITCHER
2. CATCHER
3. 1st BASEMAN
4. 2nd BASEMAN
5. 3rd BASEMAN
6. SHORTSTOP
7. LEFT FIELDER
8. CENTER FIELDER
9. RIGHT FIELDER
10. UMPIRE

HOME RUN

STRIKEOUT
HOME RUN
SPLITFINGER FASTBALL
BONUS AT BAT
PINCH HITTER
LINE DRIVE
KNUCKLE BALLS
DOUBLE STEAL

PREVIOUS PAGE, LEFT AND ABOVE

▣ BEN DRURY,
   WILL BANKHEAD

✪ HOMERUN:
   HARDFLOOR

● HARTHOUSE RECORDS

■ RECORD PACKAGE
   305 x 305 MM
   12 x 12 IN

✈ UK

D MARK TAPPIN:
BLUE SOURCE

✪ LIFE IN MONO:
MONO

● ECHO

I KATE GIBB

■ CD SINGLE SLEEVE
120 x 120 MM
4¾ x 4¾ IN

✈ UK

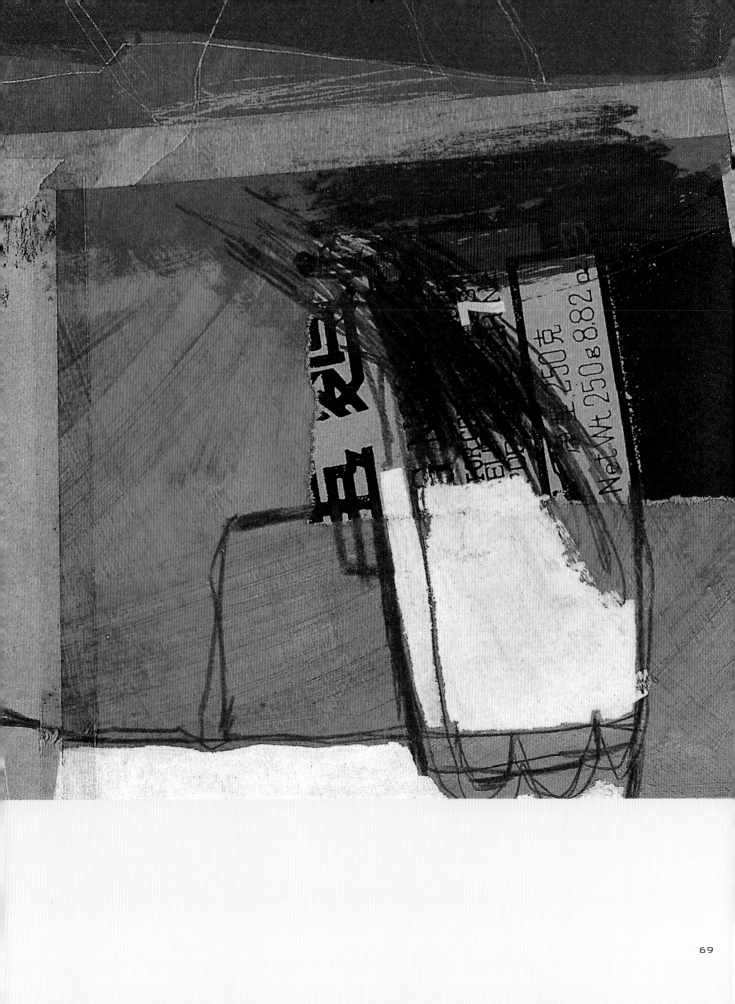

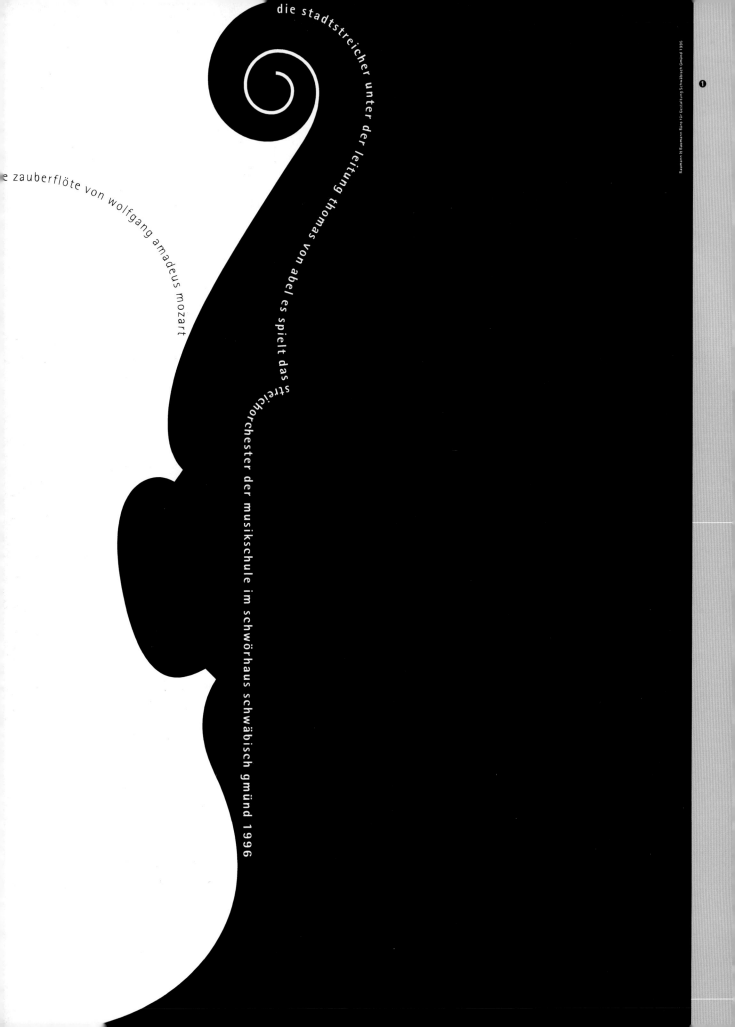

die stadtstreicher unter der leitung thomas von abel es spielt das streichorchester der musikschule im schwörhaus schwäbisch gmünd 1996

e zauberflöte von wolfgang amadeus mozart

Baumann & Baumann Büro für Gestaltung Schwäbisch Gmünd 1996

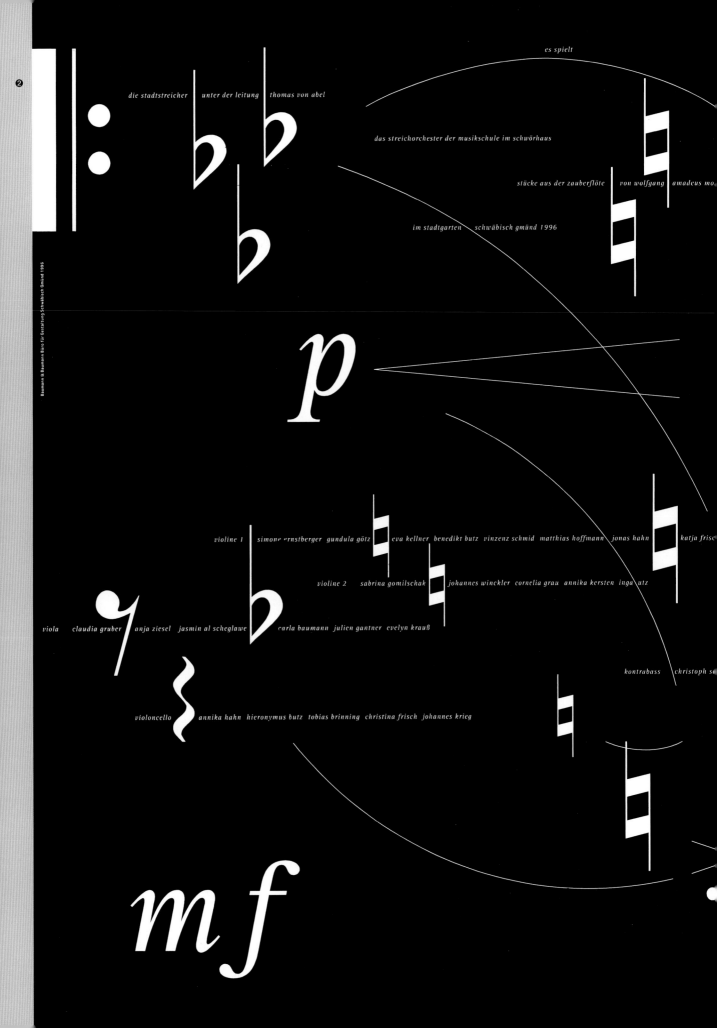

es spielt

die stadtstreicher   unter der leitung   thomas von abel

das streichorchester der musikschule im schwörhaus

stücke aus der zauberflöte   von wolfgang   amadeus mo...

im stadtgarten   schwäbisch gmünd 1996

p

violine 1   simone ernstberger   gundula götz   eva kellner   benedikt butz   vinzenz schmid   matthias hoffmann   jonas hahn   katja frisc...

violine 2   sabrina gomilschak   johannes winckler   cornelia grau   annika kersten   inga utz

viola   claudia gruber   anja ziesel   jasmin al scheglawe   carla baumann   julien gantner   evelyn krauß

kontrabass   christoph s...

violoncello   annika hahn   hieronymus butz   tobias brinning   christina frisch   johannes krieg

mf

PREVIOUS SPREAD

▣ BARBARA BAUMANN,　　● STÄDTISCHE MUSIKSCHULE, SCHWÄBISCH GMÜND
　 GERD BAUMANN:　　　■ POSTER
　 BAUMANN & BAUMANN　　840 x 694 MM
❶❷ ✪ DIE STADTSTREICHER　33⅛ x 27⅜ IN
　　　　　　　　　　　　　✈ GERMANY

PHILIPPE SAVOIR:
FILIFOX

❶ ✪ REMINISCING:

❷ ✪ IN TEMPO:
ORCHESTRE NATIONAL DE JAZZ

● VERVE/POLYGRAM S. A. FRANCE
Ⓟ CONCEPT TV/DANY GIGNOUX
■ CD CONCERTINA
✈ FRANCE

❶

REMINISCING
ORCHESTRE NATIONAL
DE JAZZ
Laurent Cugny

Cet album
est dédié au
lion.
This recording is dedicated to the lion.

532 437-2

❷

IN TEMPO
ORCHESTRE NATIONAL
Laurent Cugny
DE JAZZ

GUEST LUCKY PETERSON

Cet album
est dédié au
lion.
This recording is dedicated to the lion.

32 438-2

◨ PHILIPPE SAVOIR:
FILIFOX

❶ ✪ REMINISCING:

❷ ✪ IN TEMPO:
ORCHESTRE NATIONAL DE JAZZ

● VERVE/POLYGRAM S. A. FRANCE

▣ CONCEPT TV/DANY GIGNOUX

■ INSIDE OF CD CASE

✈ FRANCE

◨ PHILIPPE SAVOIR:
FILIFOX

❸ ✪ 1996 NEW YEAR CARD:
ORCHESTRE NATIONAL DE JAZZ

● ORCHESTRE NATIONAL DE JAZZ

■ CARD
186 x 290 MM
7¾ x 11⅜ IN

✈ FRANCE

❶

74

❷

③

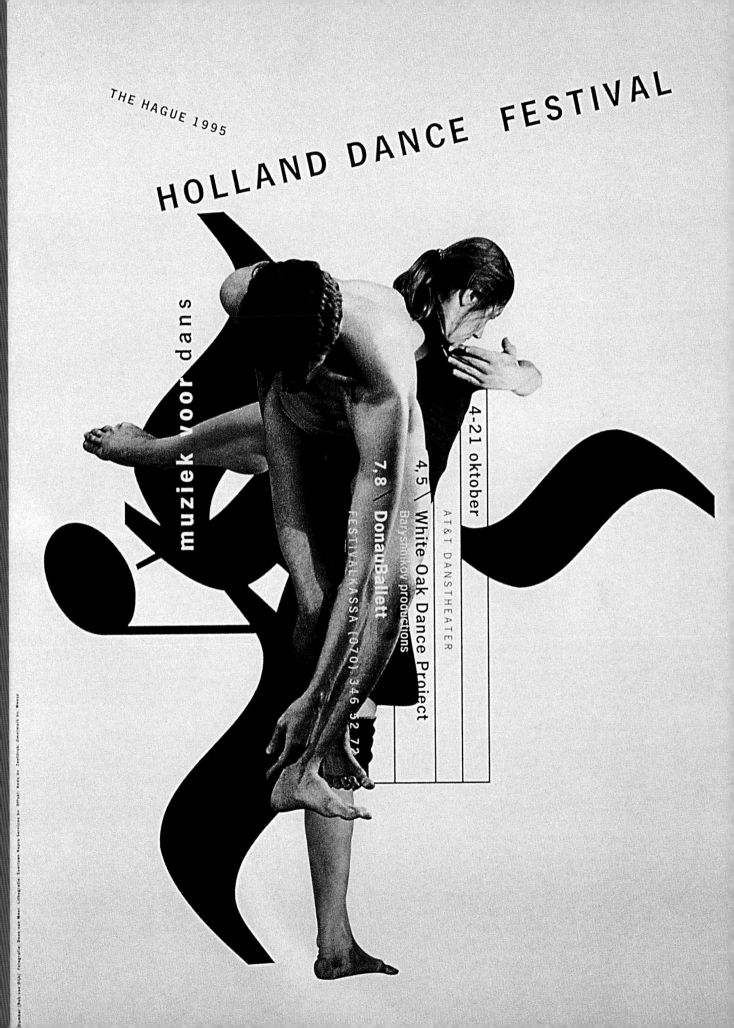

certificate of appreciation

thank you

Rock and Wrap it up! Inc.

honors

In your efforts
in helping to feed the hungry
through food pickup and sharing.

Rock and Roll has a conscience and you are it.

Syd Mandelbaum, Founder

Date

❶

we are grateful to you

for your participation
in feeding those that hunger.

Rock and Wrap It Up!, Inc.
Syd Mandelbaum, Founder

For more information on how to contribute,
please call us: 1 800 791 4064
or e-mail: ruler@delphi.com

PREVIOUS SPREAD

◨ BOB VAN DIJK:
STUDIO DUMBAR

✪ HOLLAND DANCE FESTIVAL

▣ DEEN VAN MEER
■ POSTER
168 × 117 MM,
6⅝ × 4⅝ IN

✈ THE NETHERLANDS

◨ RESA BLATMAN:
RESA BLATMAN/BELLA DESIGN

✪ FEED THE HUNGRY:
CHARITY EVENT

● ROCK & WRAP IT UP, INC.

▣ RESA BLATMAN

❙ RESA BLATMAN
■ CERTIFICATE OF APPRECIATION
203 × 254 MM
8 × 10 IN
❶

■ CARD
143 × 111 MM,
5¼ × 4⅝ IN
❷

✈ USA

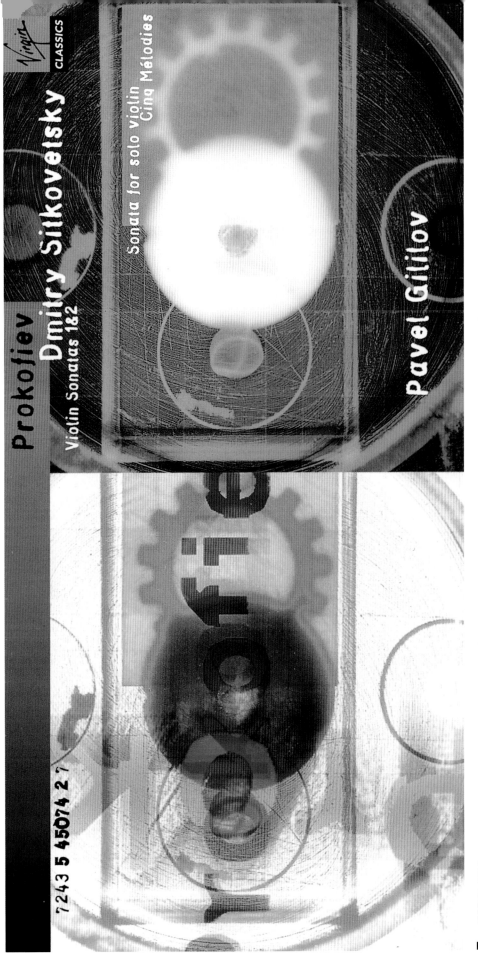

Virgin CLASSICS

Prokofiev

Dmitry Sitkovetsky

Violin Sonatas 1&2

Sonata for solo violin
Cinq Mélodies

Pavel Gililov

7243 5 45074 2 7

◄ JEREMY HALL

▣ JOEL RAJWADI,
LINZI BARTOLINI:
RED ROVER

✿ PROKOFIEV:
VIOLIN SONATAS 1 & 2:
DMITRY SITKOVETSKY,
PAVEL GILILOV

● VIRGIN CLASSICS
▣ JOEL RAJWADI
■ CD COVER
✈ UK

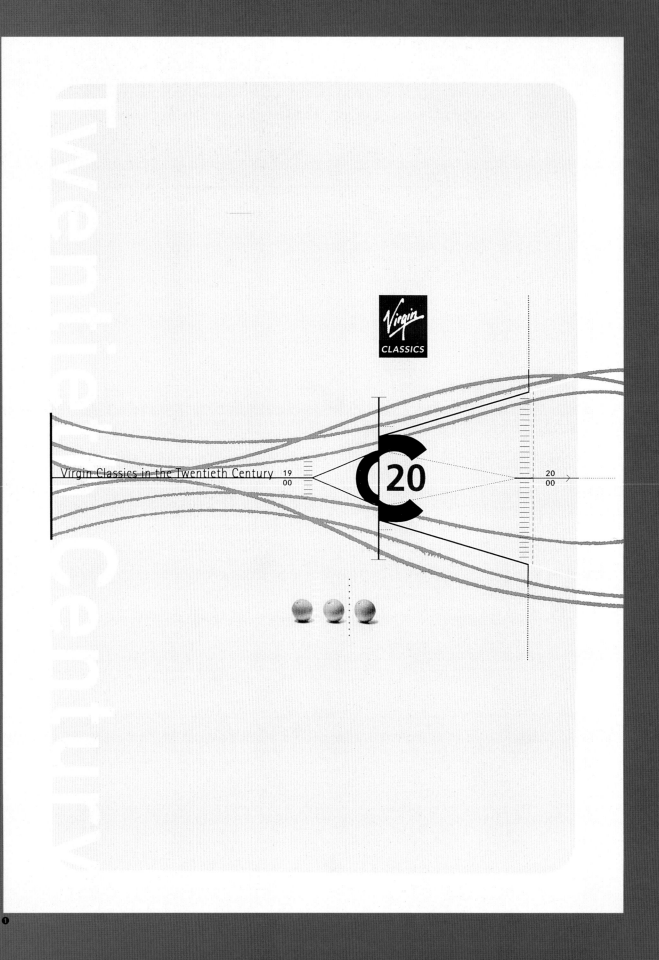

Virgin Classics in the Twentieth Century

❷

Brahms | GRIEG TRIO

Piano Trios   *opp. 8 & 87*

❸

A STEFAN SAGMEISTER
D STEFAN SAGMEISTER,
VERONICA OH:
SAGMEISTER INC.

✪ MOUNTAINS OF MADNESS:
H. P. ZINKER
● ENERGY RECORDS
P TOM SCHIERLITZ
■ INSIDE OF CD CASE
✈ USA

A ▣ STEFAN SAGMEISTER
D ▣ STEFAN SAGMEISTER,
VERONICA OH:
SAGMEISTER INC.

✪ SET THE TWILIGHT REELING:
LOU REED
● WARNER BROS RECORDS INC.
℗ TIMOTHY GREENFIELD SANDERS
▬ TONY FITZPATRICK
■ CD CONCERTINA
✈ USA

KEY TO SYMBOLS USED IN CAPTIONS

▲   Art Director
◨   Designer(s): Design company
✪   Title: Artist
●   Record label/client
▣   Photographer(s)
◼   Illustrator
◼   Description and dimensions*
✈   Country of origin

*NOTE
All CD covers, booklets, fold-out
concertinas, cases, and packages
are a standard size of 120 x 120 mm
(4¾ x 4¾ in) unless otherwise
specified. All album sleeves are
a standard size of 305 x 305 mm
(12 x 12 in).

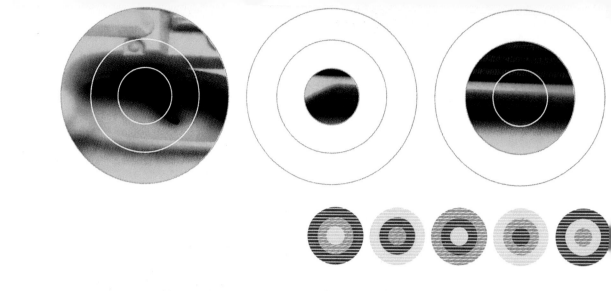

!K7®
387.10073
K7R007CDM
LC 7306

TERRENCE PARKER Pure Disco

K 7 R 0 0 7 c d

📺 MARC SCHILKOWSKI

❶❸ ☆ PURE DISCO:

❷❹ ✲ TRAGEDIES OF A PLASTIC
SOUL JUNKIE:
TERRENCE PARKER

● K7 RECORDS

■ CD COVER, CD

✈ GERMANY

❷

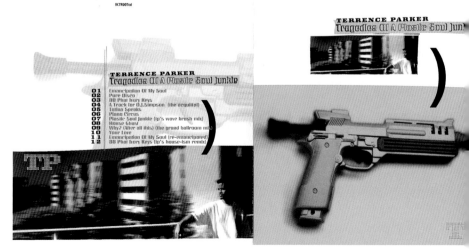

!K7R007cd

TERRENCE PARKER
Tragedies Of A Plastic Soul Junkie

01 Emancipation Of My Soul
02 Pure Disco
03 88 Phat Ivory Keys
04 A Track for O.J.Simpson (the acquittal)
05 Tatiua Speaks
06 Piano Circus
07 Plastic Soul Junkie (tp's wave brush mix)
08 House Guest
09 Why? (After all this) (the grand ballroom mix)
10 Your Love
11 Emancipation Of My Soul (re-emancipated)
12 88 Phat Ivory Keys (tp's house-ism remix)

TERRENCE PARKER
Tragedies Of A Plastic Soul Jun

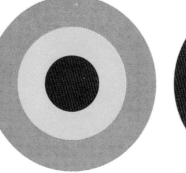

1 Pure Disco
2 88 Phat Ivory Keys
3 Emancipation Of My Soul (re-emancipated)
4 Plastic Soul Junkie

All songs written, arranged, produced, mixed and conceived by Terrence Parker 4 Seven Grand Productions.
Published by EMI (Benelux) /Seven Grand Publishing /BMI(Rest of the World) Licensed from Intangible
Records. Design: Marc Schilkowski
All rights reserved. Unauthorized copying, reproducing, hiring, lending, public performance and broadcasting prohibited.
℗+© STUDIO K7 1996 !K7 Records is a division of STUD!O K7, Leipzigerstr. 54, 10117 Berlin, Fax
+49-30-2044456 e-mail K7@contrib.de

TERRENCE PARKER Pure Disco K 7 R 0 0 7 C D M

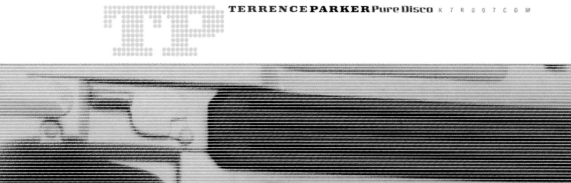

❸

❹

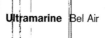

Ultramarine | Bel Air

Produced and engineered by Ultramarine at Nu Kross, South London.
All tracks written by Ian Cooper and Paul Hammond
except tracks 2, 5, 10 and 16 by Cooper/Hammond/Pooka.
Additional musicians: voices and lyrics - Pooka (Sharon Lewis and Natasha Jones), double bass - Dave
Green, vibes - Roger Beaujolais, trumpet - Del Crabtree.

Design and art direction: Substance,
(Chris Ashworth, Neil Fletcher, Amanda Sissons).
Photographic images: John Holden.

Contact: Ultramarine information c/o Freepost CV744,
3 Alveston Place, Leamington Spa, CV32 4BR, UK.
E-mail: amigos@ultramarine.co.uk

Love and thanks - Sharon and Natasha, John and Chris,
Jim @ Pathway, Jones, Alison, Jane, Adrian, Emily, Simon.

And to all our friends - past, present and future...
greetings from bel air.

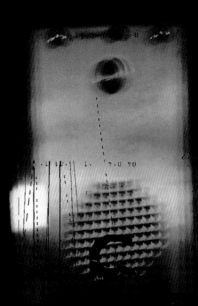

Ultramarine | Bel Air

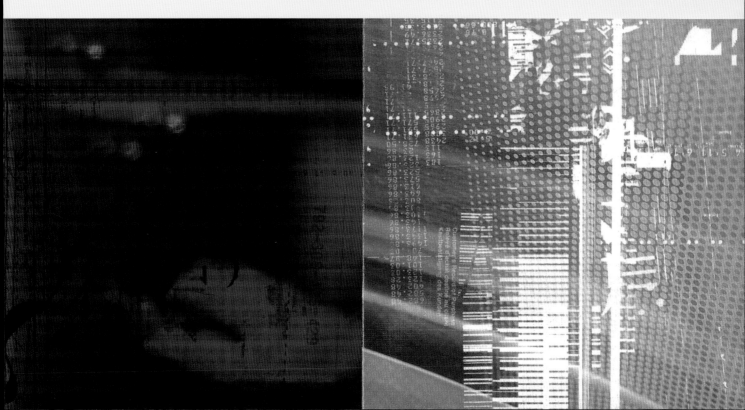

SPOT SATELLITES > LAUNCHED BY ARIANE ROCKET > ORBITING @ 830KM

THE OFF-WORLD COVER GRAB IS NOT A PHOTOGRAPH > SPOT ON BOARD DETECTORS MANIPULATE VISUAL & INFRA-RED LIGHT

trance.house@n

ABDUCTION IS CONCEIVED AND COMPILED BY TOM PARKINSON AND RUPERT LORD FOR SOLID STATE RECORDS > A&R/LICENSING BY TIM BINNS > ART DIRECTION BY LEX MURRAY > SLEEVE BY PETER CHADWIC

LICENSED IN ASSOCIATION WITH HARD HANDS, WARNER MUSIC/PERFECTO, JUNIOR BOYS OWN, SONY MUSIC ENTERTAINMENT, R&S RECORDS, LIMBO RECORDS, REACT MUSIC, LOADED RECORDS, WARP RECOR
DECONSTRUCTION/BMG RECORDS, PLATIPUS RECORDS, LOGIC RECORDS, POLYGRAM/FFRR/INTERNAL, SINEWAVE US, DRAGONFLY RECORDINGS/BIG LIFE

THANKS OUT THERE TO LISA @ HARD HANDS, JULIE, KATHY, RICK & TONIA @ WARNERS, KATHY & SONYA @ XL, ALAN & CLARE @ SONY, KAREN, KATHY & LUCY @ POLYGRAM, LUC @ R & S, MAGGIE @ LIMBO, MC
FENELLA, TONY & DOUG @ LOGIC, VANESSA @ SYNEWAVE, JERRY, CHARLOTTE & JANE @ HOOJ, PAUL @ DECONSTRUCTION, JOHN @ PLATIPUS, KAY @ REACT, JC @ LOADED, LUCY @ JBO & GREG & ROB @ WARP

NOT FORGETTING THE VITAL CREW > IAN DUTT > TONY DUCKWORTI

D   PETER CHADWICK:
     ZIP DESIGN

✪   ABDUCTION:
     VARIOUS ARTISTS

●   SOLIDSTATE

P   SCIENCE PHOTOGRAPHIC LIBRARY, UK

■   CD CONCERTINA,
     INSIDE OF CD CASE

✈   UK

abduction

ABDUCTION

A COMING TOGETHER OF QUALITY EURO-TRANCE AND HARD HOUSE

SOLIDSTATE ▷

UNMIXED TWIN CD

ED BY DICK BEETHAM @ TAPE II TAPE

RECORDS, EYE Q MUSIC, XL RECORDINGS, HOOJ CHOONS
@ MUSHROOM, DARREN @ DRAGONFLY. SARAH @ BIG LIFE
@ ROHAN MEDIA & SPOT IMAGE/SCIENCE PHOTO LIBRARY

THE ROAD > TELESALES AND ALL AT VITAL DISTRIBUTION

50 3261200022 7

30 TRACKS INCLUDING   SALT TANK   THK   LEFTFIELD   JAM & SPOON
LEMON INTERUPT   GOLDEN GIRLS   MARMION   BT   WAY OUT WEST   GYPSY
WIPPENBERG   SUBLIMINAL CUTS   HARDFLOOR   POLTERGEIST   VERNON   HAVANA
LI KWAN   PUMP PANEL   JAYDEE   JUNGLE HIGH   REMAKE   ZODIAC YOUTH

trance.house@newstate.demon.co.uk

T DIRECTION BY LEX MURRAY > SLEEVE BY PETER CHADWICK @ ZIP > MASTERED BY DICK BEETHAM @ TAPE II TAPE

RECORDS, REACT MUSIC, LOADED RECORDS, WARP RECORDS, INFECTIOUS RECORDS, EYE Q MUSIC, XL RECORDINGS, HOOJ CHOONS
LIFE
Y & LUCY @ POLYGRAM, LUC @ R & S. MAGGIE @ LIMBO, MOIRA @ EYE Q. ANDY @ MUSHROOM, DARREN @ DRAGONFLY. SARAH @ BIG LIFE
REACT, JC @ LOADED. LUCY @ JBO & GREG & ROB @ WARP, DC @ PURE. ZOE @ ROHAN MEDIA & SPOT IMAGE/SCIENCE PHOTO LIBRARY

T FORGETTING THE VITAL CREW > IAN DUTT > TONY DUCKWORTH > SALES BODS ON THE ROAD > TELESALES AND ALL AT VITAL DISTRIBUTION

SOLIDCD2 50 3261200022 7

abduction

2CD > 30 TRACKS > ABDUCTION SOLIDCD2

abduction

91

THIS IS EASY

iT IS REFRESHINGLY DIFFERENT, QUITE FASCINATING AND THOROUGHLY ENJOYABLE FROM START TO FINISH

EASY

52 FIRST CLASS **PERFORMANCES** WITH **CRYSTAL CLEAR** STEREO SOUND

FEATURING
BURT BACHARACH
HENRY MANCINI
DIONNE WARWICK
ESQUIVEL
JOHN BARRY
GEOFF LOVE
RAY CONNIFF
BJ THOMAS
TONY HATCH
COUNT INDIGO

STEREO

❶

THIS IS THE **RETURN OF** **CULT FICTION**

36 CULT CLASSIC FILM & TV THEMES

STARSKY & HUTCH
ENTER THE DRAGON
RETURN OF THE SAINT
THE PROFESSIONALS
SIX MILLION DOLLAR MAN
CHARLIE'S ANGELS

TAXI
WONDERWOMAN
NORTH BY NORTHWEST
MINDER
MAN ABOUT THE HOUSE
VISION ON
FLY ME TO THE MOON
ON THE BUSES
SKI SUNDAY
WHITE HORSES
TALES OF THE UNEXPECTED

❷

🄳 PETER CHADWICK:
ZIP DESIGN

❶ ✪ THIS IS EASY:
VARIOUS ARTISTS

● VIRGIN RECORDS

🄿 TOPHAM PICTURE LIBRARY

■ CD COVER

❷ ✪ THIS IS THE RETURN
OF CULT FICTION:
VARIOUS ARTISTS

● VIRGIN RECORDS

🄿 FORD PHOTOGRAPHIC
ARCHIVE

■ CD COVER

✈ UK

VICD 112 7243 8 42166 2 7

GROOVE

CD TWIN-SET FOR THE TOMORROW GENERATION

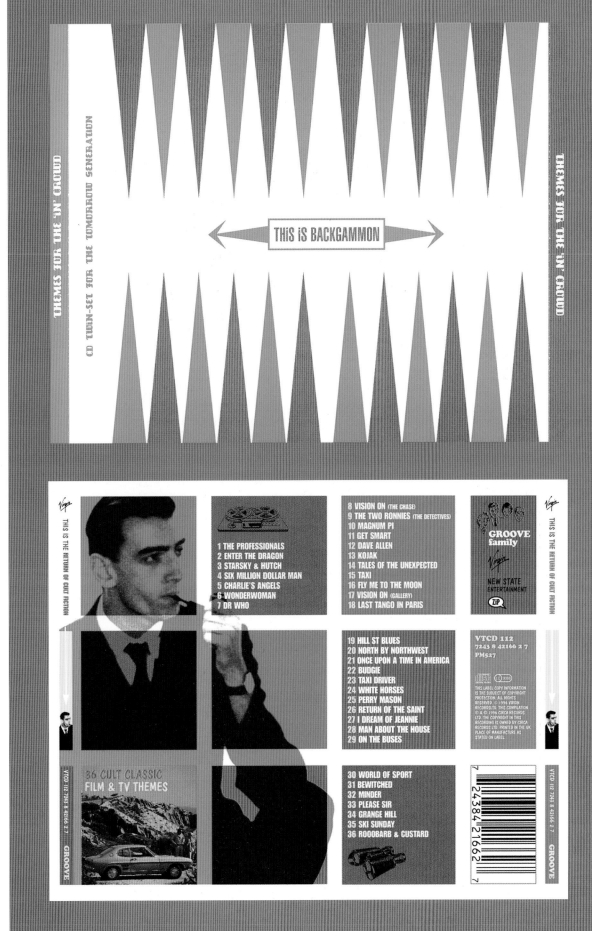

THIS IS BACKGAMMON

THIS IS THE RETURN OF CULT FICTION

GROOVE family

NEW STATE ENTERTAINMENT

ZIP

THIS IS THE RETURN OF CULT FICTION

1 THE PROFESSIONALS
2 ENTER THE DRAGON
3 STARSKY & HUTCH
4 SIX MILLION DOLLAR MAN
5 CHARLIE'S ANGELS
6 WONDERWOMAN
7 DR WHO

8 VISION ON (THE CHASE)
9 THE TWO RONNIES (THE DETECTIVES)
10 MAGNUM PI
11 GET SMART
12 DAVE ALLEN
13 KOJAK
14 TALES OF THE UNEXPECTED
15 TAXI
16 FLY ME TO THE MOON
17 VISION ON (GALLERY)
18 LAST TANGO IN PARIS

19 HILL ST BLUES
20 NORTH BY NORTHWEST
21 ONCE UPON A TIME IN AMERICA
22 BUDGIE
23 TAXI DRIVER
24 WHITE HORSES
25 PERRY MASON
26 RETURN OF THE SAINT
27 I DREAM OF JEANNIE
28 MAN ABOUT THE HOUSE
29 ON THE BUSES

30 WORLD OF SPORT
31 BEWITCHED
32 MINDER
33 PLEASE SIR
34 GRANGE HILL
35 SKI SUNDAY
36 ROOOBARB & CUSTARD

VTCD 112
7243 8 42166 2 7
PM527

THIS LABEL COPY INFORMATION IS THE SUBJECT OF COPYRIGHT PROTECTION. ALL RIGHTS RESERVED. © 1996 VIRGIN RECORDS LTD. THIS COMPILATION ℗ & © 1996 CIRCA RECORDS LTD. THE COPYRIGHT IN THIS RECORDING IS OWNED BY CIRCA RECORDS LTD. PRINTED IN THE UK. PLACE OF MANUFACTURE AS STATED ON LABEL.

36 CULT CLASSIC FILM & TV THEMES

VTCD 112 7243 8 42166 2 7   GROOVE

VTCD 112 7243 8 42166 2 7   GROOVE

7 24384 21662 7

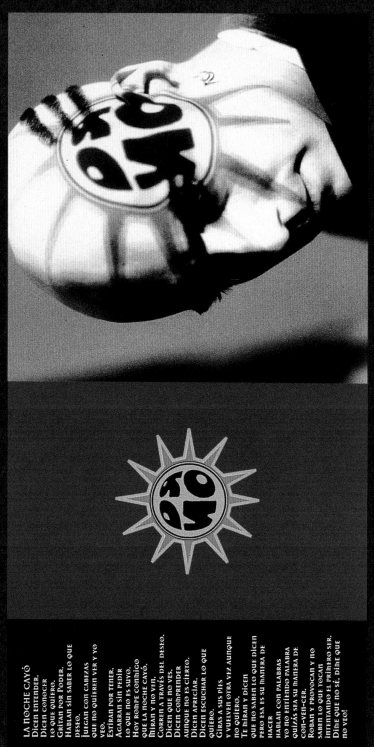

PADECHU D'BOUE

LA NOCHE CAYÓ
DICEN ENTENDER,
DICEN CONOCER
LO QUE QUIERO,
GRITAN POR PODER,
HABLAN SIN SABER LO QUE
DESEO.
JUEGAN CON CABEZAS
QUE NO QUIEREN VER Y YO
VEO.
ESTIRAN POR TENER,
AGARRAN SIN PEDIR
LO QUE NO ES SUYO,
HOY ROMPE CONMIGO
QUE LA NOCHE CAYÓ,
MIRAN Y NO VEN,
CORREN A TRAVÉS DEL DESEO.
DICEN QUE NO VES,
DICEN COMPRENDER
AUNQUE NO ES CIERTO.
DICEN APRECIAR,
DICEN ESCUCHAR LO QUE
QUIERO,
GIRAS A SUS PIES
Y VUELVEN OTRA VEZ AUNQUE
NO QUIERO,
TE MIRAN Y DICEN
QUE NO SABEN LO QUE DICEN
PERO ESA ES SU MANERA DE
HACER
HABLAN CON PALABRAS
YO NO ENTIENDO PALABRA
QUIZÁS SEA SU MANERA DE
CON-VEN-CER.
ROBAN Y PROVOCAN Y NO
SABEN LO QUE TOCAN
INTENTANDO EL PRIMERO SER,
DIME QUE NO SÉ, DIME QUE
NO VEO!

D DAVID RUIZ:
  MARINA COMPANY
✪ DR NO:
  DR NO
● SONY MUSIC
P AGUSTIN VALLE
■ CD COVER,
  BOOKLET
✈ SPAIN

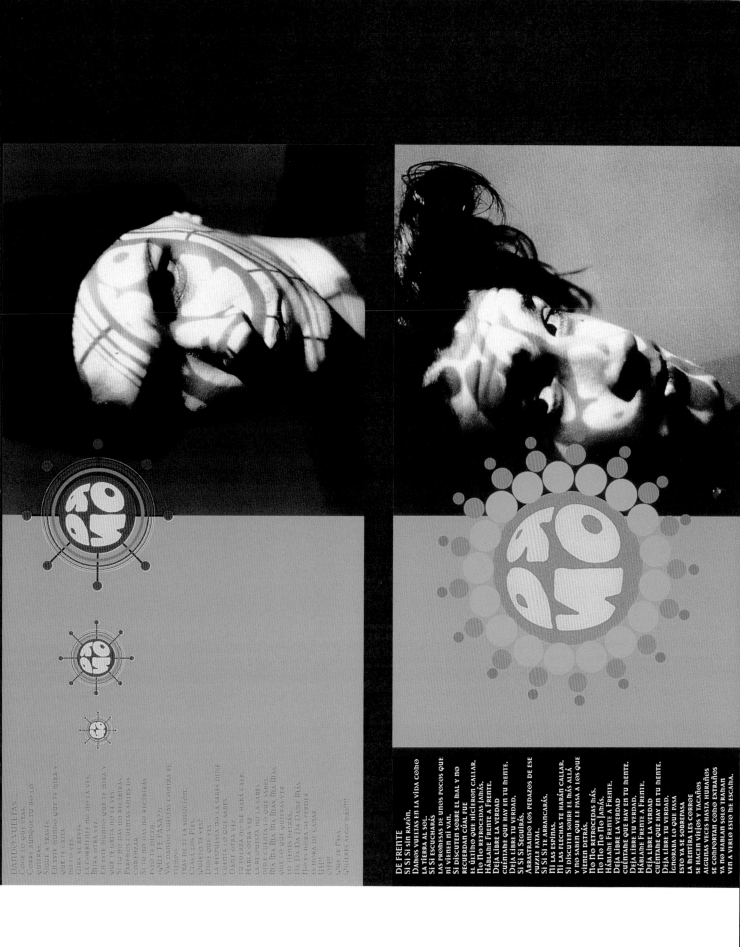

DANDO VUELTAS...
Coge lo que sea,
Corre, aunque tú no lo
quieras.
Sigue a través,
En este bullebulle que te mira,
quieras, quieras.
No lo ves.
Gira al revés,
La corriente no no la ves.
Tira otra vez,
En este bullebulle que te mira y
que te gira no lo ves.
Si tú no das no no mira,
Párpeos ocultas antes de
comenzar.
Si tú no vas no no verás
Esto te digo
(¿Que te pasa?)
Va dando vueltas contra el
tiempo
Una de ti la solución,
Clava los pies,
Quieto te ves?
Dile qué ves
La respuesta no la sabrás dime
Cuenta lo que sabes
Tira otra vez.
La respuesta me hará caer
Habla otra vez
La respuesta no la sabes,
Date cuenta lo que sabes,
Bla bla bla bla bla bla bla bla bla
Que lo que quieras ver
No tienes piernas,
Da da da da dame más.
No es hora de perder.
Es ahora de caer
Uhh
Ohh
Que te pasa,
Quizás algo más???

DE FRENTE
Si si si sin razón,
Damos vueltas en la vida como
la tierra al sol,
si si escucharás
las promesas de unos pocos que
ni vienen ni van,
si discuten sobre el mal y no
recuerdan cuál fue
el último que hicieron callar.
No no retrocedas jamás,
Háblame frente a frente.
Deja libre la verdad
Cuéntame que hay en tu mente.
Deja libre tu verdad,
Si si si seguirás.
Arrastrando los pedazos de ese
puzzle fatal.
Si si si te arrancarás,
ni las espinas,
ni las flechas te harán callar.
Si discuten sobre el más allá
y no saben que te pasa a los que
vienen detrás.
No no retrocedas más,
No no no no jamás,
Háblame frente a frente.
Deja libre la verdad
Cuéntame que hay en tu mente,
Háblame frente a frente.
Deja libre tu verdad,
Deja libre la verdad
Cuéntame que hay en tu mente,
Deja libre tu verdad,
Ignora lo que pasa
Esto ya se sobrepasa
La mentira les corroe
Se hacen viejos y tacaños
Algunas veces hasta huraños
Se comportan como extraños
Ya no hablan solo tratan
Ven a verlo esto me escama.

Infinite Studio, un lab
grafica, tipografica e fot
Ad Infinite Studio si
innovative per l'immagi
della musica e dell'ente

**Compact disc, cofane
speciali, edizioni lim
cassette, libri, realiz
supporti per i punti v
ideazione di merchan
pagine web, Cd -Rom,
coordinamento d'imm**

La filosofia di **Infinite**
partner ideale per chi è
dimensione artistica d'c
produzioni musicali, edi
dell'immagine di prodo

Infinite Studio ha con
Excellence" 1997 per il
conseguente inserimente
Regional Design Annual
rivista americana Print.

❶

❷

Infinite Studio, ideato e diretto da **Fabio Berruti**. L'attività di fotografo e grafico che svolge da oltre dieci anni, passando attraverso molteplici campi di applicazione della comunicazione visiva, è sfociata nella fondazione del laboratorio di idee Infinite Studio.

Infinite Studio
è ad Albisola
fuori dal centro
al centro del mondo

via casarino, 127
17013 **albisola superiore** (savona)
tel 0**19 48 82 37**
fax 0**19 48 49 51**
e mail **infinite@mbox.it.net**

▣ FABIO BERRUTI:
    INFINITE STUDIO

❶ ✺ PROMOTIONAL LEAFLET:
    INFINITE STUDIO

🅿 FABIO BERRUTI

■ LEAFLET
    150 X 210 MM
    5⅞ X 8¼ IN

❷ ✺ E YA PO:
    GIANNA NANNINI

● GIENNE PUBLISHER

🅿 GUIDO HARARI/NANNINI ARCHIVE

■ FANZINE FOR THE
    GIANNA NANNINI FAN CLUB
    155 X 210 MM
    6¼ X 8¼ IN

✈ ITALY

PREVIOUS SPREAD

✺ INFINITE STUDIO CALENDAR 1997

🅿 FABIO BERRUTI

■ PROMOTIONAL CD CALENDAR
    120 MM DIAMETER
    4¾ IN DIAMETER

✈ ITALY

rapporto tra lei e il pubblico tedesco.
alle 11 e 40 Gianna Nannini con un commando di Greenpeace, imbragata con una ... si fa issare sul balcone del piano nobile di Palazzo Farnese, sede dell'ambasciata ...gna un microfono e si scatena in un concerto. L'esibizione-blitz dura mezz'ora e si con... nna che si asciuga il sudore nella bandiera francese. È l'azione più eclatante portata a ...eenpeace in Italia. Un atto di protesta contro la decisione del governo francese di riprendere i ...teori nell'atollo di Mururoa.

...: "Ottava vita", obiettivo, remixarla, mischiandone ancora una volta di più i suoi conte-culturali. Il risultato è ottimo: il remix, ha sonorità dure e martellanti, senza nessun sapore ...che non sovrastano mai il testo della canzone. Anzi, lo rafforzano, rendendolo ancora ...penetrante. Un vero e proprio "excursus" - anche culturale e sociale - tra i balli e le musi-...oggi, italiane e internazionali, europee ed extraeuropee.
Gianna partecipa a vari Festivals in Europa, tra i quali quello di Nyon come "head-liner" ...utta italiana (oltre a lei ci sono i Mau Mau e Paolo Conte). In platea ci sono oltre 45.000 ...a sale sul palco alle 23.15 e per più di due ore dà vita ad uno spettacolo di grande energia. ...bre 1995: Gianna è al Festivalbar. Da Lignano Sabbiadoro a Marostica, sino alle finale ... - ad Ascoli Piceno, dove riceve il premio per il Miglior Tour Estero.
...5: La giunta comunale di Verona rischia di spaccarsi per "colpa" di Gianna. Il motivo? ...a cultura ha deciso di offrire alla città - il 6 settembre a piazza S. Zeno, di fronte alla ...oncerto gratuito della Nannini, ma una parte della giunta si oppone per via del "carat-...ello show" (è un concerto antinucleare, sostenuto da Greenpeace). la "querelle" come ...su tutti i giornali ! Alla fine, comunque, il concerto si farà. Sono presenti oltre 20.000

...995: dal Palasport di Genova parte la tournée italiana di Gianna contro il nucleare . Lo ...iamoci con la musica, no al nucleare". Il pubblico, numerosissimo, è tutto con lei. A ...sta magica serata arriva alle 23.39, dieci minuti dopo la fine dello show, la notizia che ...o appena effettuato il 1° test nucleare a Mururoa. La lotta va avanti, più decisa che mai.
...995: nella piazza dell'Università di Torino va in scena un concerto per niente comune. Gianna ...i Timoria, Nomadi e un coro di 16 monaci tibetani. È stato un incontro casuale con ...Thamthong Rinpoche a farle conoscere la "questione tibetana" e a farle venire l'idea di invitare in Italia un coro di monaci tibetano per una serie di spettacoli di musica sacra. Un evento spirituale e culturale, certo, ma anche un modo concreto per raccogliere fondi per il monastero tibetano di Sera Je.
16 settembre 1995: davanti ad oltre 30.000 perso-ne si chiude a Napoli, dopo aver toccato le princi-pali città e aver coinvolto oltre 180.000 persone, il tour di Gianna. Il tema della serata è l'immigrazio-ne. Lo show, infatti, rientra nel "Progetto Villa Liternio" voluto dal Forum Antirazzista della Campania, il consorzio Pitré (Paolo Rossi, Serena Dandini, Stefano Benni, l'Arcivescovo di Caserta, il sindaco di Napoli, Bassolino, e il senatore verde Luigi Manconi. Il Progetto - nato per creare intorno agli immigrati di Villa Liternio una rete di solidarietà e di sostegno non occasionale - ha dato vita ad una sottoscrizione per finanziare un progetto di ristrutturazione di edifici desti-nati ad alloggi e ad un centro di incontro per immigrati. Un progetto preciso, quindi, che però si stacca dal suo microcosmo per diventare una provocazione generale, rivolta a tutti. Un invito chiaro e deciso alla solidarietà, quella vera. Un altro atto d'a-more di Gianna.

THE GREATEST HITS COLLECTION

BOMBOLONI

29 agosto

anno 2 - numero 2
luglio 1996

è ya po
e ya po TUTTE MUSICA
e ya po E non MUSICA

numero 2

BOMBOLONI

❷

❶

▣		MARTIN VENEZKY
❶	✪	REPRISE – THE NEXT GENERATION: VARIOUS ARTISTS
	●	REPRISE RECORDS
	℗	MARTIN VENEZKY
	■	CD COVER 127 x 130 MM 5 x 5⅛ IN
❷	✪	SPEAK 2: VARIOUS ARTISTS
	●	ISLAND RECORDS
	■	CD COVER, CD
❸	✪	SPEAK: PREVIEW ISSUE
	℗	MELODIE MCDANIEL
	■	MAGAZINE COVER 254 x 305 MM 10 x 12 IN
	✈	USA

❷

FASHION AND MODERN CULTURE

SPEAK

BOWL-O- RAMA

BOO RADLEYS

CHELSEA HOTEL
REVISITED

TINDERSTICKS
MIAMI'S LAST
HOLDOUT

JIMMY SMITH
BIRDS OF
VENICE

FOU -COLOR
PRINTING
+
+
+
+
+
MOR
E

PREVIEW
ISSUE
$3.95 U.S. $4.95 CANA
DA

"CONCENTRATE
ON
SUCCESS"

who is this mild-mannered, haired, resident who turns into the Tasmanian devil of the turntables? He deconstructs beats, putting them back together in syncopated rhythm with

one of rap music's most influential figures, Kool DJ RED ALERT is neither a rapper, musician, manager or producer. He is a radio personality, but one who speaks fewer words on the air in a year than Howard Stern says in an hour. That's because his mouth isn't what makes Red Alert special: it's his ears

who is red-
fem
who is

by Dimitri Ehrlich

mic instincts to rival those of a master percussionist. And he is arguably the subject of more recorded shout-outs than anyone else in the world, hence his nickname "the Prop Master." Red gets his propers from hundreds of emcees who owe him their first play, or simply respect his skill, his sensibility, and his staying power in an industry where three albums makes you a veteran. Over the course of a decade, he's been the first radio DJ to play dozens of hip-hop records that went on to become national hits. He has also been among the bravest and most eclectic programmers, mixing everything from Hall & Oates, Men At Work, and the Rolling Stones into a rap show known for its unassailable underground credibility (tapes of his shows circulate on the street for as much as $25 each.) "I try to keep my ears clean," says Red, "and listen for sounds that are different from others and can help lead off."

Red also helped lead the rise of dancehall reggae, mixing rap's Jamaican counterpart into his shows as early as 1988. Last year he released an album for Epic Records entitled Kool DJ Red Alert's Dancehall Show, showcasing new dancehall talent, including Vicious, who went on to release a successful solo album. "A lot of people credit me for playing dancehall reggae. I took a risk on it because Afrika Bambaataa showed me that you can combine any kind of music with hip-hop and rap sounds. But I had learned about this music anyway, before reggae; I had learned soca, calypso and meringue from my grandparents who come from Antigua."

Red began his career under the tutelage of one of rap's founding fathers, a Bronx-based Jamaican-American named Kool Herc, who knew about the dance hall reggae sound systems in Kingston. It was there that Jamaican emcees, known as toasters, began to develop their rapid patois boasting in the 1970s, around the same time that rap, dancehall's American cousin, was developing in New York City clubs such as Pippins, Superstar Cafe, and the Diplomat Hotel. There, Red heard pioneering DJs like the late Grandmaster Flowers, the late Charisme, Pete "DJ" Jones, Together Brothers, and, in the Bronx, Kool Herc. As disco and funk collided, Red Alert found his calling in the emergent music then called "hip-hop/bebop." In 1979 he joined Afrika Bambaataa's legendary Zulu Nation, as part of a

group called Soulsonic Force. "There was a club called the Twilight Zone up on Jerome Avenue in the Bronx," says Red. "I came in there and it was like a whole different scene, because Herc was DJing and mixing the records back and forth, instead of one after the other. And that's what inspired me." By 1983, Red began broadcasting his own hip-hop show, he has since released several what he has to the hundreds of demo tapes and records that he receives every week and he still lives in his parents' home on 113th Street. "I still live in the same neighborhood, still tend to people the same way. I feel better that way because I feel you'll be more respected when people see you don't change. A lot of people expect you to be fancy, riding big cars, living in a big house. I don't think that really gives you respect. Just remain as you are."

And what does the hip-hop avatar see for the future of the genre? Rap radio's least talkative DJ isn't telling. "You got to go with the people that create it. You can't say it, but you can play it."

MARTIN VENEZKY

SPEAK: PREVIEW ISSUE

PAIGE STUART, TAR

MAGAZINE SPREAD

254 X 305 MM

10 X 12 IN

USA

by Dimitri Ehrlich

temperature

BUT he's funkier than your little brother's gym socks, and here's how you know: take the funk taste test. Grab a copy of Damn! (Verve), the veteran jazz/funk/R&B organ-player's most recent album, and compare it to the latest by BRAND NEW HEAVIES, US3, or any other new jack acid jazz group you care to imagine. Notice how Smith sounds *lovely* like butter and the competition seems like pure Parkay by comparison?

Here's what matters: *burning*. There are hot organ solos and then there are hot organ solos, and then there's Jimmy Smith. Smith plays the second kind. When Smith gets cooking on one of his infamous solos, it sounds as though he were hacking away at the keys of his organ with a fierce axe, simultaneously dousing his rotating Leslie speaker with gasoline and setting the beast ablaze. Fluid, lyrical improvisations skate across the keys with amazing grace, and then attack you sideways, with Smith's trademark percussive rabbit-punch style. It can all be very dizzying as a listening experience, but it's also elegant, robust, and never too hoity-toity.

Marking Smith's return to Verve after a 23-year absence, Damn! features a host of jazz's young lions, including trumpeter Roy Hargrove, bassist Christian McBride, and guitarist Mark Whitfield, none of whom were born when Smith scored his first great successes in the mid 1950s and early 1960s. "This is more exciting than the old sessions," Smith says. "You're working with young guys, 22 or 23 years old, and they've mastered their horns already. It scares me that they know all these things. Some of these guys have 'testified me with the go."

Smith covers a range of modern black music, from James Brown's classic "Papa's Got a Brand New Bag" to Dizzy Gillespie's hard-bobbing "Woody 'N' You." Damn! also features two of the greatest drummers of all time, the ubiquitous Bernard Purdie, and the late Arthur Taylor, who contributed the final B-3 performances of his lifetime to the recording.

Herbie Hancock, (whose jittery aplomb and one of the lightest, loosest and juiciest grooves of the last 10 years) Smith does not pander to the beats and music that came after him. While Hancock's most recent album, Dis Is Da Drum got lost in mish-mash of contemporary loops and drum programming, Smith delivers the goods in a raw, timeless fashion. You won't confuse his sound for that of any of Smith's many imitators because he doesn't try to give it a '90s spin. He's smart. With so many bands sampling him and struggling to cop that furious and famous Jimmy Smith Style, why would he try to emulate them?

And if anyone ever tells you they don't like jazz because it's too stodgy or fancy or old-fashioned, do them a favor. Lay some Jimmy Smith on them. And watch their head start to rock, and their eyes start to smile, and their mouths start to say,

Born in Norristown, Pennsylvania, on December 8, 1928, James Oscar "Jimmy" Smith was nine years old the day he won first place on Major Bowes Amateur Hour radio show, playing boogie woogie piano. "I had piano books on the underneath me so I could reach the keys," Smith recalled of that seminal moment. "Once I got going, I didn't want to stop. The announcer was saying, 'Ladies and gentlemen, this kid's on fire. He's burning the place up.'" Many years later, after a stint in the navy, Smith was playing with the R&B group one saxophonist suggested when he first laid his hands on something called a Hammond B-3. It was a Hammond B-3, to be precise. It was a very mean machine. He says he borrowed money from a loan shark to buy his first Hammond B-3. It was a deal made with the devil. *But it didn't matter.*

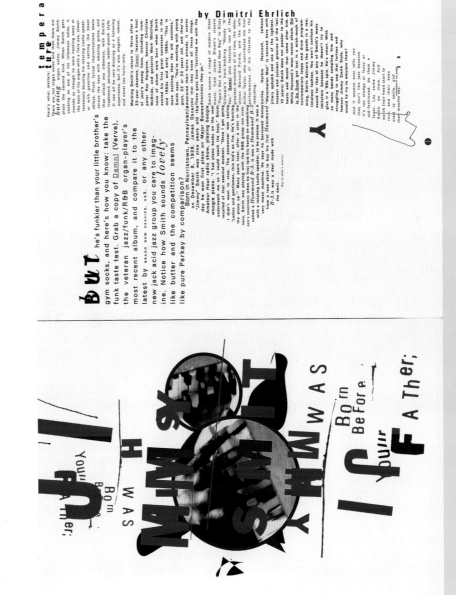

OVERLEAF

MICHAEL FAULKNER: RAW PAW GRAPHICS

CHIAROSCURO

SCURO

D-FUSE

SLIDE PROJECTION USED AS BACKDROP IN CLUB

35 MM SLIDE

UK

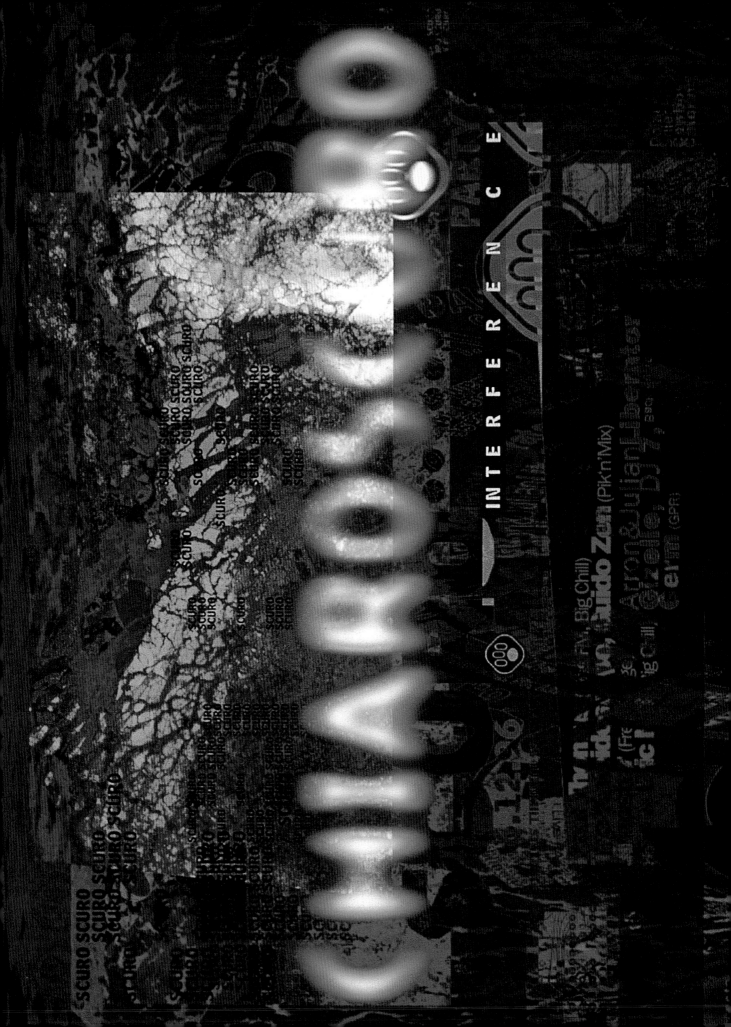

EIKE KÖNIG:
EIKES GRAFISCHER
HORT

YOUR HOUSE
IS MINE:
ASTROSYN

EVERYONE HAS
INSIDE:
GALA

ORBIT RECORDS/
VIRGIN RECORDS

EIKE KÖNIG

CD COVER

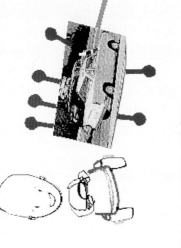

740 BOYZ FEAT. 2 IN A ROOM: SHIMMY SHAKE   579 905-2

740 BOYZ feat. 2 IN A ROOM
SHIMMY SHAKE

79 905-2

ⓒ 6748

400 HZ

1. L.2 MIX   06.07
2. A.B MIX   06.43
3. A.B QUINTET MIX   06.24
4. TORRENT UNDERGROUND MIX 06.40

400hz
I'VE GOT THE MUSIC IN ME

400 HZ   I'VE GOT THE MUSIC IN ME   577 653-2

7 653-2

▲ EIKE KÖNIG

▣ EIKE KÖNIG,
MARCO FIEDLER:
EIKES GRAFISCHER
HORT

✕ BUMP BUMP/
PARTY OVER HERE/
SHIMMY SHAKE:
① 740 BOYZ

▣ CHRISTIAN LANTRY

✕ I'VE GOT THE
MUSIC IN ME:
② 400 HZ

▬ MARCO FIEDLER

● SUBURBAN/
MOTOR MUSIC/
POLYGRAM

■ CD COVER
✈ GERMANY

107

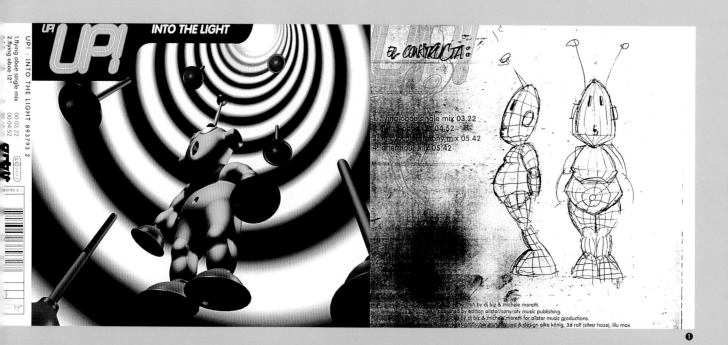

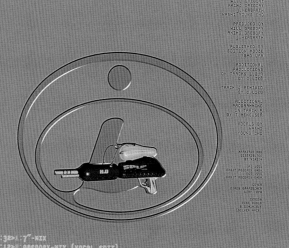

⬛ EIKE KÖNIG:
EIKES GRAFISCHER HORT

❶ ✪ INTO THE LIGHT:
UP!

⬤ ORBIT RECORDS/VIRGIN RECORDS

▮ MAX, RALF HIEMISCH

◼ CD COVER

❷ ✪ DUM DUM DABADA:
BOOMBASHI

⬤ ORBIT RECORDS/VIRGIN RECORDS

▮ DOMINIQUE

◼ CD COVER

❸ ✪ MOTOR:
VARIOUS ARTISTS

⬤ MOTOR MUSIC/URBAN

ℙ EIKE KÖNIG

◼ PROMOTIONAL ADVERTISEMENT
210 X 297 MM
8¼ X 11¾ IN

✈ GERMANY

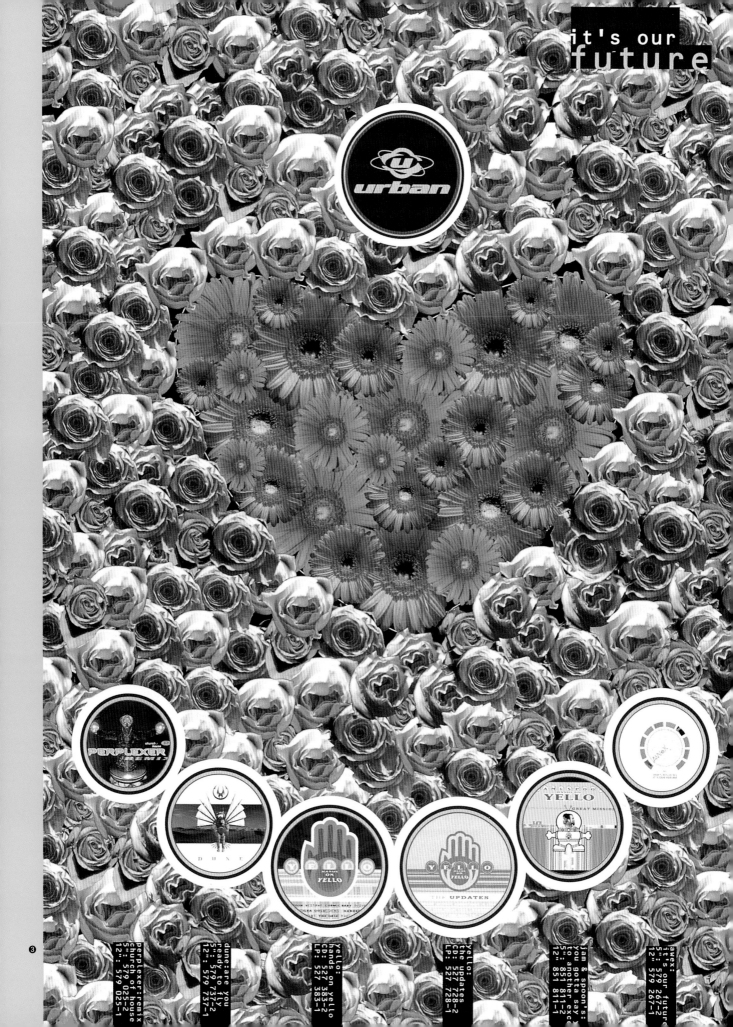

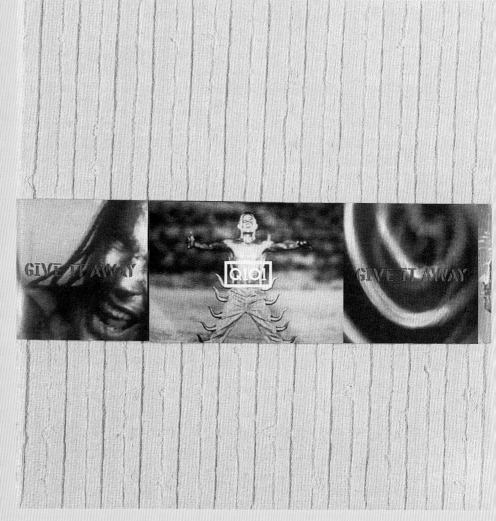

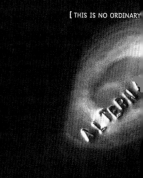

[THIS IS NO ORDINARY

WIN A TRIP AT THE Q101 PARTY!

BELLY UP TO THE BAR WITH US ON **WEDNES**
FROM 5:30 PM UNTIL 10 PM AT OUR FAVORITE POOL HA

ATTENDANCE IS MANDATORY. COME AN
WHILE. WE'LL GIVE IT AWAY ALL NIGH
AND, YEAH, A QUAINT, LITTLE JAUNT A
TO WITNESS THE RED HOT CHILI PEP

PLEASE LET YOUR INTENTIO
RSVP ASAP TO LSJS (LA 'SHAWN J. SANDI

◰ CARLOS SEGURA:
   SEGURA INC.

✪ GIVE IT AWAY:
   RED HOT CHILI PEPPERS

● Q101 RADIO

■ INVITATION
   127 x 127 MM
   5 x 5 IN

✈ USA

we're gonna GIVE IT AWAY!

MBER 27, 1995
EST INSTITUTE PLACE.

IT WORTH YOUR
, BALLS, STICKS—
ANTIC FOR TWO

MILAN, ITALY.

5-1253. CIAO

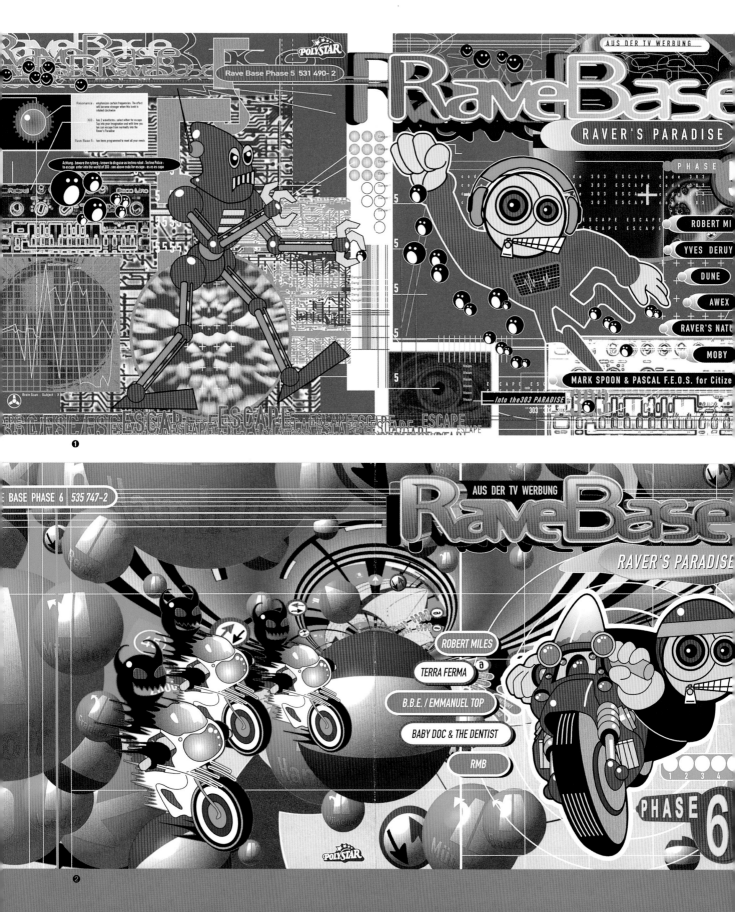

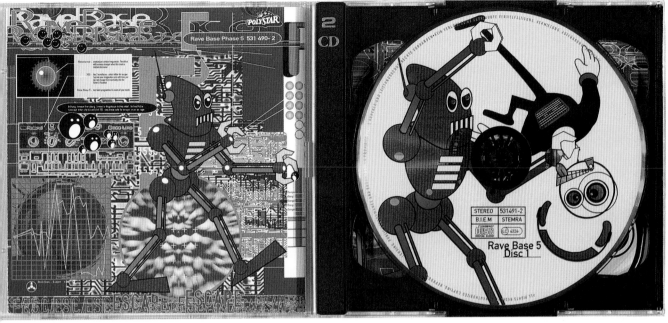

❶

❷

A	PETER HAYWARD
D	PETER HAYWARD, ED HOLDING: MAINARTERY
❶ ★	RAVER'S PARADISE – PHASE 5:
❷ ★	RAVER'S PARADISE – PHASE 6: RAVE BASE
●	POLYSTAR/POLYMEDIA
■	CD COVER, INSIDE OF CD CASE
✈	UK

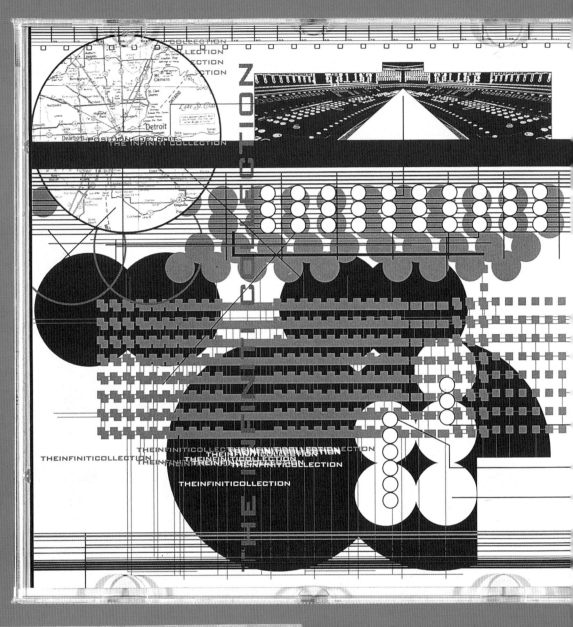

PETER HAYWARD:
MAINARTERY

INFINITI COLLECTION:
JUAN ATKINS

TRESOR, BERLIN

CD COVER,
INSIDE OF CD CASE

UK

SANDOZ **every man got dreaming**

1.1 **morning star**
2.1 **heist** | 2.2 **sniper**
3.1 **future past**
4.1 **shadowmask** | 4.2 **glass factory** | 4.3 **the wreckers**

All tracks written arranged and produced by RH Kirk for Intone Productions.
Recorded and mixed at Western Works Studios, Aug / Sept 95.
℗&© 1995 Touch. Copyright control.
Cover image: Phil Barnes. Design: Eg.G.

Touch, 13 Osward Road, London, SW17 7SS. Tel: +44 181 767 2368.
Distribution: UK: Kudos / Pinnacle. USA: Dutch East India Trading.
Semaphore, Andernacherstrasse 23, 90411 Nurnberg, Germany.
Tel: +49 911 952770. Fax: +49 911 9527750.

TECHNICAL DATA

D DOM RABAN:
EG.G

★ EVERYMAN GOT DREAMING:
SANDOZ

● TOUCH

I PHIL BARNES

■ RECORD SLEEVE
305 x 305 MM
12 x 12 IN

✈ UK

1.1 LOST SOULS ON FUNK
1.2 LOVE IS DEEP
1.3 SO DIGITAL

2.1 INDOLE RING
2.2 EAST OF NIMA
3.1 ATOMIC
3.2 POETS SAINTS REVOLUTIONARIES

4.1 MONOCHROME DREAM
4.2 THE NUMBER OF MAGIC

WRITTEN ARRANGED AND PRODUCED BY R H KIRK FOR INTONE PRODUCTIONS PUBLISHED WARP MUSIC / EMI MUSIC. RECORDED AND MIXED AT WESTERN WORKS STUDIOS DEC 94 / FEB 95. MASTERED BY GEORGE PECKHAM @ PORTS THANKS TO ROB STEVE KEV/R NANCY EMMA AND CHANTAL AT WARP ℗ © 1995 WARP RECORDS

COVER IMAGE: PHIL BARNES. DESIGN / COLLAGE: Eg.G ORIGINAL PHOTOGRAPHY: LYNNE CLARK

D DOM RABAN:
EG.G

✪ THE NUMBER OF MAGIC:
R. H. KIRK

● WARP RECORDS

P LYNNE CLARK

I PHIL BARNES

■ RECORD SLEEVE
305 x 305 MM
12 x 12 IN

✈ UK

▣   DOM RABAN:
     EG.G

✪   THE NUMBER OF MAGIC:
     R. H. KIRK

●   WARP RECORDS

▣   LYNNE CLARK

▣   PHIL BARNES

■   INSIDE OF RECORD SLEEVE
     680 x 305 MM
     26¾ x 12 IN

✈   UK

□ LILLY TOMEC

❶ ✪ CLOSER TO REALITY:
LOOPHOLE
● AMBER RECORDS/POLYDOR
℗ DINAH FRANK, LILLY TOMEC
■ CD COVER
140 x 125 MM
5½ x 4⅞ IN
✈ GERMANY

❷ ✪ T.O.T.:
LOOPHOLE
● AMBER RECORDS/POLYDOR
℗ XAVIER 2 NAUW, DINAH FRANK, LILLY TOMEC
■ CD COVER
140 x 125 MM
5½ x 4⅞ IN
✈ GERMANY

LOOPHOLE
Closer To Reality

LOOPHOLE Closer To Reality

1 Radio Edit   3:59
2 Best Boy Electric Mix   4:24
3 T-Power Mix   7:07
4 Nightmare On Wax Mix   5:51
5 Bad Boy Electric Mix   5:34
6 Best Boy Electric Mix (Extended Version) 6:02
7 BBE Juggler Mix   5:59

LOOPHOLE

t.o.t.

amber

LOOPHOLE t.o.t

531 596-2

1. Closer To Reality 5:46
2. I, Me & Mine 4:20
3. Times Of Trouble 6:20
4. Hocus Pocus 0:50
5. Oh Please, Oh Please 4:45
6. Sentimental Lover 5:26
7. Beauty Fool 3:56
8. A New Loophole 6:08
9. Children 4:05
10. Satisfied 4:57
11. We Can Try 4:32
12. Relationships 6:33

Polydor

AMBER Records is marketed by Polydor.

© 2001 Amber Records GmbH
© 2001 Polydor GmbH
Brockengartenwall 3
20095 Hamburg
Distributed by Polygram

for more information:
Amber Records
Fax: +49-30-215 50 68
e-mail: dobie@berlin.snafu.de
homepage! www.amber.de

LC 4611
PY 900
CD 531 596-2
BIEM/STEMRA

7 31453 15962 4

OVERLEAF

🄳 LILLY TOMEC
✸ CLOSER TO REALITY: LOOPHOLE
🅿 AMBER RECORDS/POLYDOR
● DINAH FRANK, LILLY TOMEC
■ CD BOOKLET
140 x 125 MM
5½ x 4⅞ IN
✈ GERMANY

531 596-2

Dobra Publishing/BMG UFA.
Oh Please, Oh Please published by Budde Musikverlag, Warner Chappell,
All Tracks published by Warner Chappell and Dobra Publishing/BMG Ufa except
R. Walton, A. Toma
Relationships written by C. Mayfield, D. Nkishi,
R. Walton, A. Toma
Oh Please, Oh Please written by G. Kerr, D. Nkishi
except:
All tracks written, arranged & produced by Loophole
Loophole are: Dodo Nkishi, Raoul Walton, Andi Toma

I WILL TAKE THE CONSEQUENCES.

IN TIMES OF TROUBLE

When really hungry, longing 4 your daily bread,
You need ONE, 2 show you how life Should be led,
Who's with you when nobody else helps you find
                        that precious peace of mind.
If you feel lonely & forgotten & this world appears
                        2 eat you up &
When even you stab your Self in the back, there's
    some ONE else, you can always check.
    Dark is the night, so stormy is the weather
But there is a way, if you will it, you will ease
                        the pressure.
So, do it right, get your self to gather, for
  wether right or not, you must live 4 ever.
  2 be guided & protected with the ONE you must
                        be connected.
   Ain't no use to choose 4ce or 2th, just the ONE
      (is the ONE!) who is gonna turn you loose –
                        when you feel bK>

vocals: Dominique Nkishi
supporting vocals: Jupp Götz,
Felicia Uwage, Donna Renee,
Andi Toma, Dominique Nkishi
piano: Sascha Kühn
bass: Raoul Walton
programming: Raoul Walton,
Andi Toma

HOCUS POCUS
programming: Andi Toma

vocals: Dominique Nkishi
supporting vocals: Jupp Götz, Andi Toma,
Dominique Nkishi
accoustic guitar: Dominique Nkishi
bass: Raoul Walton
programming: Andi Toma

OH PLEASE, OH PLEASE (JUST ONE MORE CHANCE)

Isn't it funny how the consequence doesn't make sense
till experienced?
When things have really gotten out of hand, then down we
bend on our knees & cry!
But what had happened cannot be undone, so stop regret-
ting & accept you had fun.
Time is ticking on & on & maybe one day you'll be
forgiven. But now you cry, but don't deny, it's your
life, make your choice well.
Imagination you must have got, to think that you could
live your life like that.
Taking & taking it for granted that there will always be
a "next time" ahead.
Taking & taking, but never give. Taking & making it like
a thief.
Now you better think of this one: Last, the time before
the last was your last! And now you cry, don't deny,
whether you live with love or strife.
You built your life on what you were built; living is
dying, for life to be build. Again & again the cycle
repeats: You build your life on what you were built.

SENTIMENTAL LOVER

Sentimental lover, you have always been
longing for another act to stage your
scene. Cause you must dramatize & every
mood helps to entize your cast to follow
you straight to those tear drops in your
eyes.
Living like you're driven only by your
passion, you made an impression on my mind
as if you just never knew the con-sequen-
ses of your indiscretion. But I keep trying to find why it is that you will miss
to give your self the blame for your
depression. But I just do not know!? Life
is big, — so big! we cannot pretend to
know what is best for all of us.
Sentimental lover, now you realize, men
like me don't bother; we're as cold as
ice. So well you judge my kind to be
thoughtless, to be blind, of the dearest
wishes pricking your mind.
If I would find a Lady's — slipper, you
wouldn't mind if I would rip her off; just
for you! Or a little furry pet, of those
I bet I could not get enough. Maybe you
will make a deal with me, if I agree your
bid for love? But I don't think so. Like
an unquenchable fire, your desires burn
inside your heart.

vocals: Dominique Nkishi
supporting vocals: Felicia Uwage,
Donna Renee, Dominique Nkishi
viola: Axel Ruhland
guitar: Dominique Nkishi
bass: Raoul Walton
drums: Dominique Nkishi
programming: Andi Toma

A NEW LOOPHOLE

TRAVEL — to the deepest regions
of your mind. TRAVEL — see what
you can find.
Read what it says on that tag:
„Welcome friend you have just
been sent to a new Loophole.
When you found what you must
find, find your goal! When you
go back don't pretend you have
invented it all — for there was,
there is & always will be a new
Loophole!!!"
TRAVEL to the edge of anything &
you will find a space. Truth is
always inbetween & under the
surface.
TRAVEL to the edge of thought &
you will find a gap. Look at it
a little closer, you will find a
tag; read what it says on that
tag: „welcome, friend you have
just been ...!!!"

vocals: Dominique Nkishi
supporting vocals: Donna Renee,
Raoul Walton, Dominique Nkishi
keyboards: Raoul Walton
programming: Andi Toma, Raoul Walton

BEAUTY FOOL

I look bad now, because you made me sad, when
I felt so good with what we had. But suddenly you took me by your side, where you
let me see! I should have caught what was
coming, but hypnotized I was by your eyes.
That's when I got shot, started to loose it,
— 60 missiles sent by Mr. Cupid. Hit I was
right there, where my head usually abides.
What should I do? This was the day, when I
would say the stupidest thing, I could have
ever ...
You, see! the truth is, I went along, 'cause
I could not tell right from wrong; mama
could & dad would & all the family; but nobody tells you what they really see. So, they
all said that we were matching, when all we
really did was acting.
I played the fool, you the beauty, together
they called us Beauty Fool.
For so long you'd been waiting for a night
in shining amore. By came I, riding my
black, firm legs straight into your eye.
Quick you dressed to the very best, looking
at me just like a princess, fit for a king.
You made your hips swing! There was surely
no way of escaping; I was taken, my body sha-
ken, sweating & aching, till I did awake.
Than the realization, I was only dreaming,
got me screaming of relief.

vocals: Dominique Nkishi
supporting vocals: Donna Renee,
Felicia Uwage, Maximilian Stamm,
Andi Toma, Dominique Nkishi
piano, wurlitzer: Xaver Fischer
guitar: Andi Toma
bass: Raoul Walton
programming: Raoul Walton,
Andi Toma

This is a BRANDNEW WARNING in this
new age dawning, like a hurricane
destroys all that what mankind
enjoys. It beholds a message which
is so profound, higher than the
highest skies & lower than the
lowest ground.
It will shake you up from bottom
to the top & it won't stop, till
finally you accept it & give up.
CHILDREN — WE COME TO BE
BECOME — REALITY
SO LONG — MISERY
WELCOME — SPIRITUALITY
Now, you might have a difficulty
to see what it means, to be forever happy, when you're free from
what is transitory. But with ease
you will find pleasure from wordly
kind only to see, forever & again
you will get left behind.
Realize! Don't be surprised, it's
just life. But, yet! Never forget
you are in disguise.
CHILDREN — WHO COME TO BE
BECOME — REALITY
SO LONG — MISERY
WELCOME — SPIRITUALITY

vocals: Dominique Nkishi
supporting vocals: Dominique Nkishi
piano, wurlitzer: Xaver Fischer
bass: Raoul Walton
programming: Andi Toma

vocals: Dominique Nkishi
supporting vocals: Jupp Götz, Felicia Uwage,
Donna Renee, Dominique Nkishi
piano, wurlitzer: Xaver Fischer
bass: Raoul Walton
programming: Andi Toma, Raoul Walton

SATISFIED (NEVER, EVER)

We might not live long
enough; men & women, —
stronger! — could not
withhold their passions.
Blinded to the facts, we
continue to search for
satisfaction from this world
to quench our every urge,
just to be satisfied ...
Whole-heartedly deluded!
Intelligence, — here! — is
excluded subject to our
freedom, ever since we knew
that we can do what we may
choose. We are humans, —
that is true —, but were you
ever ...??
There is more to life than
you can imagine, you
take what you can get; look
at the earth in her beauty,
take her bleeding heart &
tear it completely apart.
Satisfied??

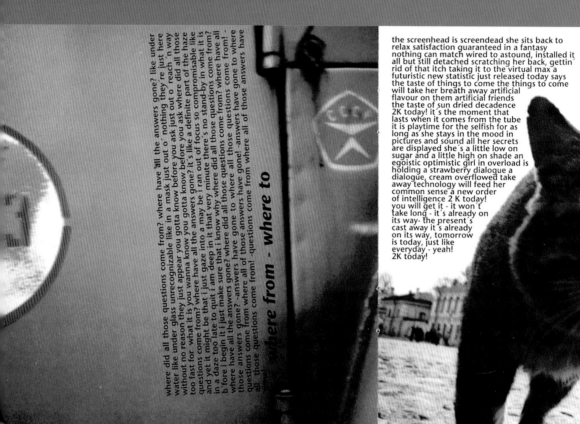

where did all those questions come from? where have all the answers gone? like under water like under glass unrecognizable like in a mask just out o´ nothing they´re just here without no reason they just appear you gotta know before you ask where did all those too fast for what it is you wanna know you gotta know before you ask it´s like a definite part of the haze questions come from? where have all the answers gone? it´s like a compromisable like and yet it might be that i just gaze into a may be I ran out of focus so compromisable like in a daze too late to quit I am deep in it that very minute there´s no stand-by in what it is b fore I begin it I just make sure that i know why where did all those questions come from? where have all the answers gone? where did all those questions come from! - where have all the answers gone? -answers have gone to where all those questions come from! - those answers come from where all of those answers have gone! -answers have gone to where questions come from where all of those questions come from! -questions come from where all of those answers have all those questions come from!

where from - where to

the screenhead is screendead she sits back to relax satisfaction guaranteed in a fantasy nothing can match wired to astound, installed it all but still detached scratching her back, gettin´ rid of that itch taking it to the virtual max a futuristic new statistic just released today says the taste of things to come the things to come will take her breath away artificial flavour on them artificial friends the taste of sun dried decadence 2K today! it´s the moment that lasts when it comes from the tube it is playtime for the selfish for as long as she stays in the mood in pictures and sound all her secrets are displayed she´s a little low on sugar and a little high on shade an egoistic optimistic girl in overload is holding a strawberry dialogue a dialogue, cream overflowed take away technology will feed her common sense a new order of intelligence 2 K today! you will get it - it won´t take long - it´s already on its way- the present´s cast away it´s already on its way, tomorrow is today, just like everyday - yeah! 2K today!

2K today

◨ LILLY TOMEC

✪ NOWHERE, NOWHERE, NOWHERE:
BIG LIGHT

● SPV HANNOVER

◧ CONCHA PRADA, SVEN HAEVSLER,
LOMOGRAPHICS, LILLY TOMEC

■ CD BOOKLET
141 X 124 MM
5½ X 4⅞ IN

✈ GERMANY

biglight.
תהגעלנעב.

no matter
where I go
no matter where i stay
moving from high to low is just a
thought away comes with company
goes with being alone feels like getting drunk
like being stoned i don't
complain, i'm liking the rain
it's just good to know why you're low
i can go anywhere and still be nowhere
no matter where i stay,
no matter where i go
doesn't take a day, to go from high
to low hail can make me laugh,
sun can make me cry
a single smile from you gets me
from low to high
i don't complain,
i'm liking the rain
it's just good to know why
you're low i can go anywhere
and still be

nowhere

the truth becomes untied now here comes the deal you know soulmates are compatible that
how i know what you feel i gotta both hands in my pockets strolling down memory lane
never time to say good bye, girl cause we're supposed to meet again i got a dream where i c
run to where words are free to fly it is my choice and i will choose you to come with me so ch
your eye in the united state of mind the united states of mind we're in the united states of m
this time every man after his fashion everyone to his taste it takes all sorts to make it happ
even the most redundant waste this offer's unrepeatable the truth becomes untied you kn
soulmates are compatible no, we couldn't lie - even if we tried in the united state of mind
united states of mind we're in the united states of mind this time my mind! - is mine! in
united state of mind the united states of mind we're in the united states of mind this time

u.s.m. (the united states of min

where from-where to
freak unique
one note symphony
... and all that gold
berlin
somehow
u.s.m.
du riechst
sister kiss
nowhere
sambanuma
2K today
exterminate all rational thoughts
don't tell a soul
pop is dead

biglight.
NowHere.NowHere.NowHere.

J. PAC
HEARTS AND FLOWERS EP
FEATURING
SHE LOVES ME

❶

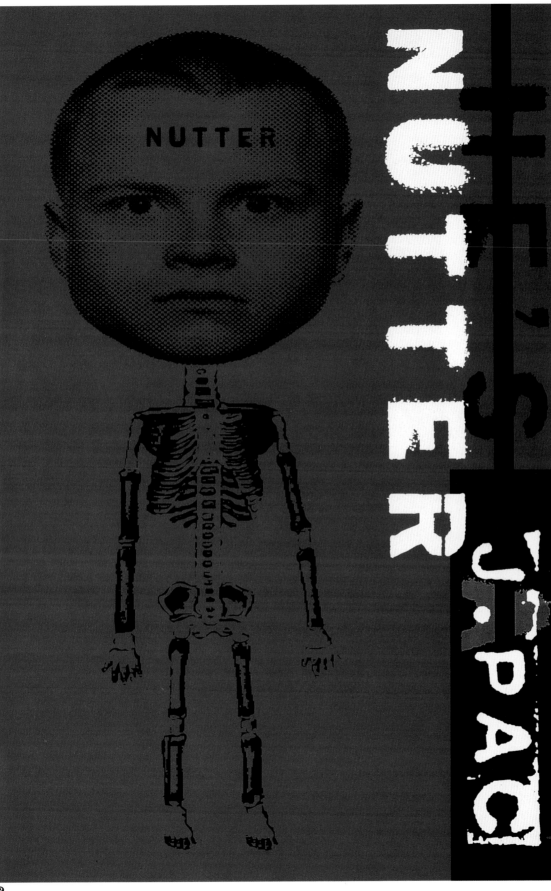

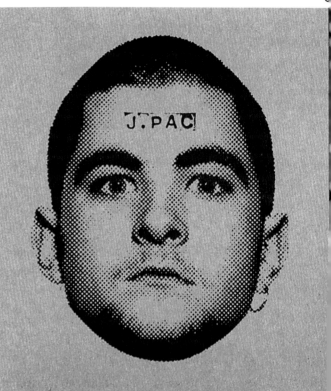

❹

EVERYTHING BUT THE GIRL
BEFORE TODAY
A1 Darren Emerson Underwater Remix 1 9.47. A2 Chicane Remix 6.74.
B1 Darren Emerson Underwater Remix 2 8.47. B2 Adam F Remix 4.12. B3 Dillinja Remix.
A1 & B1 Mixed by Darren Emerson @ Underwater Studios, Nov '96. A2 Remixed by
N Bracegirdle and L Elstob for Chicane Productions. B2 An Adam F production for EBTG.
B3 Remixed by Dillinja. Words and music by Ben Watt.
Produced by Ben Watt.
Internet: http://www.ebtg.com. Design: Form/EBTG. Pics: Juergen Teller.
Before Today is featured on the album Walking Wounded.

イービーティージー

❶

▣	PAULA BENSON, PAUL WEST: FORM

❶ ✪ BEFORE TODAY: EVERYTHING BUT THE GIRL
● VIRGIN RECORDS
℗ JÜRGEN TELLER
■ RECORD SLEEVE 305 × 305 MM 12 × 12 IN

❷ ✪ WRONG: EVERYTHING BUT THE GIRL
● VIRGIN RECORDS
℗ MARCELO KRASILCIC
■ RECORD SLEEVE 305 × 305 MM 12 × 12 IN
✈ UK

❸ ✪ THE SOUND OF VIOLENCE: PAUL
● GRAVITY
℗ AXEL TILCHE
■ RECORD SLEEVE, RECORD 178 × 178 MM 7 × 7 IN

③

②

■ SEÁN O'MARA:
XON CORP

❶❷ ✪ FRANK 44

● FRANK

🅿 SEÁN O'MARA

■ POSTER
590 × 840 MM
23¼ × 33⅛ IN

✈ UK

OVERLEAF

■ SEÁN O'MARA:
XON CORP

❸ ✪ RUI

● CLUB RUI, DUBLIN

🅸 SEÁN O'MARA

■ POSTER
590 × 840 MM
23¼ × 33⅛ IN

✈ UK

🅰 TARA BISNAUTHSING

■ SEÁN O'MARA:
XON CORP

❹ ✪ DGADGD:
THE MALCHICKS

🅿 SEÁN O'MARA

🅸 SEÁN O'MARA

■ POSTER
590 × 840 MM
23¼ × 33⅛ IN

✈ IRELAND

❶

frank
44

132

frank

2.8.96

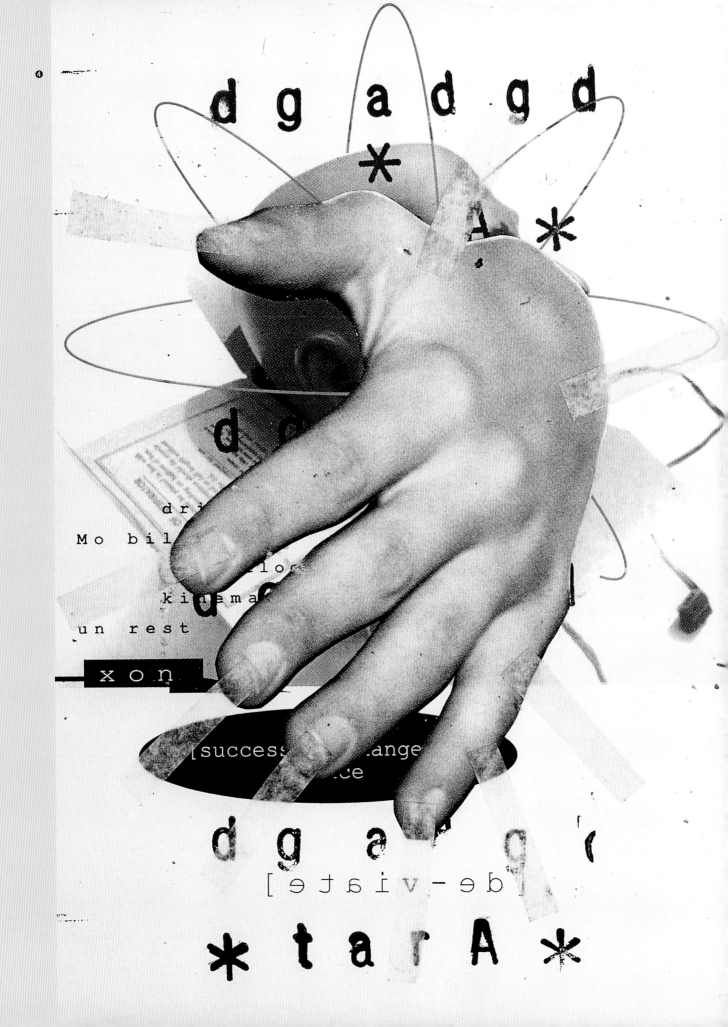

REACT REACTCD71..

Compiled by Eddie Fowlkes. A&R / co-ordination: Arul Saskia Adang. Concept inception: James Horrocks & Thomas Foley.
Thanks to: Paul Glancy, Melissa Kemp, Patrick Davis, Nicola Singh, Emma McAlister, Lewis Knott, Tina Gruneman at
React, Nicky Trax, Paul Roiz, Luke Coke, Tony, Ollie, Juan, extra special thanks to Brenda Russell & Collette Bewlis at
Phuture Trax, Nick Bax at The Designers Republic, Nikki, Alison & Terry at Tribal, Ian, Sean, Mike, Pete & all at Vital.
11: (B.Baxter) BMI. 12: (S.Echols) Santonio S/BMI. 13: (E.L.F) BMI. 14: (T.Barnett) Toronto Be-Music/BMI.
15: (K.Saunderson/Bestbeat Ltd) Chrysalis. 16: (A.Oldham) BMI. 17: (Nick Marks) Okin.
18: (James Pennington) Transmat/Mayday Music/Zomba BMI. 19: (T.Brown) BMI. 20: (Little Joe) BMG.
All tracks: ℗&©1996.

TRUE PEOPLE:
THE DETROIT TECHNO ALBUM.

REACT
REACTCD71.
Disc2.

compact
disc
DIGITAL AUDIO

11: **Blake Baxter.** Where Is The Love. 12: **Santonio Echols.** Sources.
13: **Eddie 'Flashin' Fowlkes.** T.M.F.61. 14: **Tom Barnett.** Operation-10.
15: **Kevin Saunderson. E-Dancer.** 16: **Alan Oldham.** D May 87.
17: **365 Black.** Don't Blame It On Me.
18: **Surburban Knight.** The Art Of Stalking (Remix).
19: **Tony Brown. Gama.** 20: **Little Joe.** C.R.X.

◨ THE DESIGNERS REPUBLIC

❶ ✪ TRUE PEOPLE — THE DETROIT
TECHNO ALBUM:
VARIOUS ARTISTS

⬤ REACT

🄿 ANA ADANG

◼ INSIDE OF CD CASE

✈ UK

◨ THE DESIGNERS REPUBLIC

❷ ✪ ATOM BOMB:
FLUKE

⬤ VIRGIN RECORDS

ⅠΙ D. J. ALDRED/
THE DESIGNERS REPUBLIC

◼ CD COVER
118 x 138 MM
4 5/8 X 5 3/8 IN

✈ UK

RIGHT AND OVERLEAF

D THE DESIGNERS REPUBLIC

★ PRESENT:
   SUN ELECTRIC

● R&S

P MICHAEL C. PLACE

■ CD COVER, SLIPCASE

✈ BELGIUM

TRT: 1.12.38   R & S RECORDS   THE (miT) DESIGNERS REPUBLIC   MADE IN AUSTRIA
SEE INSIDE FOR TRACKLIST   (CD) LOGO   2000.0(IRL)G :∃ϱAMI
IMAGE: G(IRL)0.0002
297.00MM(

サン・エレクトリック

SUN ELECTRIC/PRESENT
(AMB 6943 CD)

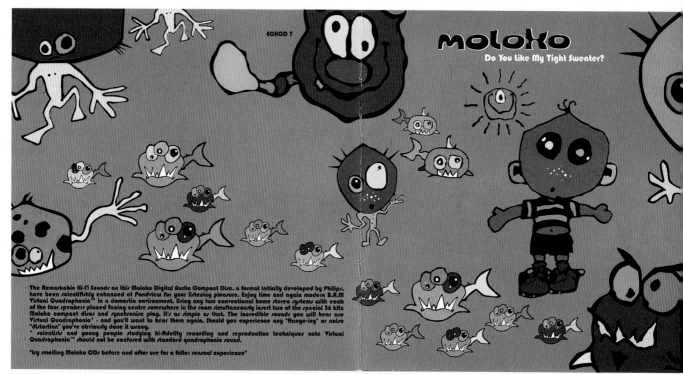

ECHCD 7

MOLOKO
Do You Like My Tight Sweater?

The Remarkable Hi-Fi Sounds on this Moloko Digital Audio Compact Disc, a format initially developed by Philips, have been scientifishly enhanced at Pondview for your listening pleasure. Enjoy time and again modern B.A.M Virtual Quadraphonia™ in a domestic environment. Using any two conventional home stereo systems with each of the four speakers placed facing centre somewhere in the room simultaneously insert two of the special 36 kHz Moloko compact discs and synchronise play. It's as simple as that. The incredible sounds you will hear are Virtual Quadraphonia* - and you'll want to hear them again. Should you experience any "flange-ing" or noise "distortion" you've obviously done it wrong.
* scientists and young people studying hi-fidelity recording and reproduction techniques note Virtual Quadraphonia™ should not be confused with standard quadraphonic sound.

"try smelling Moloko CDs before and after use for a fuller sensual experience"

killa bunnies

sniverling little bunny bouncing up and down scummy little creature run them out town in the tiny tunnels scuffling under ground toxic little bunny can always be fou danger evil rodent multiplying every day bunny taking over get on your knees a pray filthy fluffy creatures teeth as sharp as knives the longeared ones are comi run run run for your lives killa bunny is a coming killa bunny on his way killa bunny a coming are you hearing what I say

- FLUID
- WRONG SIDE OF BEAUTIFUL: DUB WAR
- EARACHE RECORDS
- CD COVER
- UK

◨ FLUID/JOHN BAKER

❶ ✿ WATAMANU:
    MOTHER

● AVEX UK/6 x 6

■ CD COVER

✈ UK

❷ ◨ FLUID

■ PROMOTIONAL PACKAGE
    223 x 140 MM
    8¾ x 5½ IN

✈ UK

❶

❷

gren

33 RPM
SIDE 1
"POP SONGS" (4:01)
WRITTEN BY White/Gonzales/Hill
PUBLISHED BY Fuzzy Melon Music/Slavey Milner
Music/Redneck Garage Sale Music/
Music Corporation of America, Inc. (BMI)
PRODUCED BY Tim O'Heir

Manufactured by I.R.S. Records, 3520 Hayden Avenue,
Culver City, CA 90232.
Warning: All rights reserved.
Unauthorized duplication is a violation of
applicable laws.
℗ & © 1995 I.R.S. RECORDS
SPRO-10742

I.R.S. RECORDS
CULVER CITY, CALIF.

This is like nothing you have ever seen – one of the most unusual and fascinating record companies in America. I.R.S. Records is a hit with native Angelenos and a treat no visitor should miss. A fashionable showcase of architectural splendor, our Culver City headquarters serves as the gathering point for a cornucopia of musical styles.

Diversity is one of our strengths – whether it's the pulsating house sound of Tribal America, artsy Gai Saber, rockin' El Dorado, worldly Hemisphere, intriguing Pangaea and Primal, or good ol' I.R.S. Records, there's sure to be something to please even the most discerning palette.

Take a stroll with us through the diverse departments that make up this musical juggernaut. From our founder Miles Copeland III and Minister of Propaganda Mike Bone down to our hardest working intern, we want to wish you a warm and festive Holiday Season. We hope you'll come by and visit us in the New Year!

Our Founder: Miles Copeland III

seasons Greetings
from I.R.S. RECORDS
3520 HAYDEN AVE.
CULVER CITY, CALIF.
90232

CULVER CITY, CALIF.

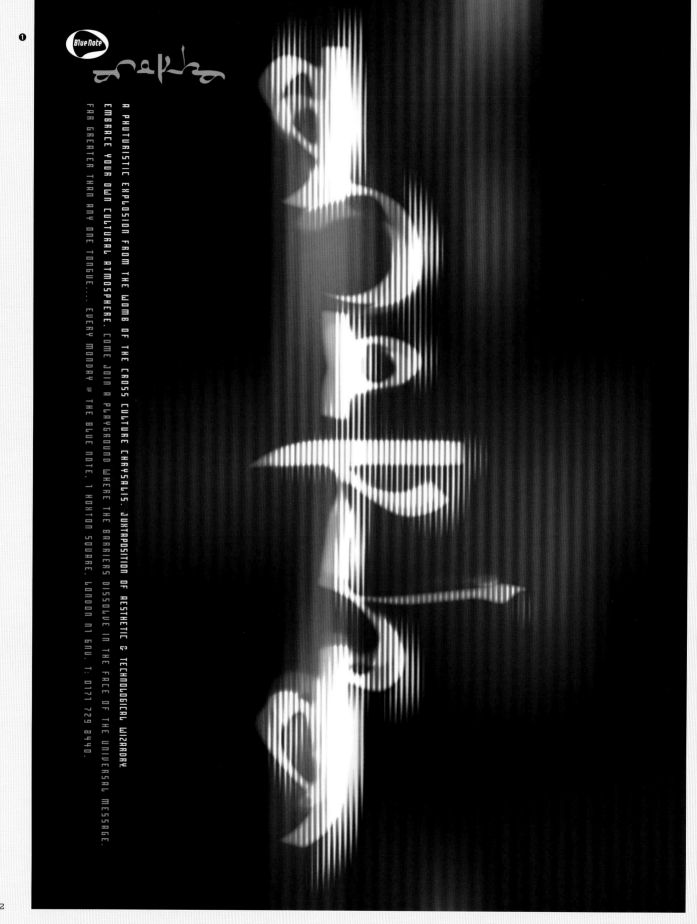

▣ TOM HINGSTON
❶ ✪ ANOKHA
● OMNI RECORDS
■ POSTER
420 x 594 MM
16½ X 23⅜ IN
✈ UK

▣ TOM HINGSTON,
ALYSON WALLER
❷❸ ✪ CLUB CULTURE
● THE BLUE NOTE CLUB
❷ ■ ALBUM SLEEVE
❸ ■ ALBUM INNER SLEEVE
✈ UK

■ SCOTT PARKER:
SOUND DESIGN

✪ SESSIONS SEVEN –
MIXED BY DAVID MORALES:
VARIOUS ARTISTS

● MINISTRY OF SOUND
RECORDINGS

℗ CHRISTOPHE DEMOULIN

■ CD BOXED SET

✈ UK

Conceived, Produced, Marketed and Agonised Over by:
Lynn Cosgrave, Clare Gage, Steve Canueto, Simon Gurney, Grace Garcia Sutcliffe, Mark Rodol, Avi Kogan, Carol Furlong and James Harris.
Compiled and Mixed by David Morales.
Mastered by Jacko at Masterpiece Mastering, London.

Special thanks to:
Judy Weinstein, Michele and all at Def Mix USA. CJ Mackintosh, Jazzy M, Frankie Foncett, Tim Deluxe, Heaven, Paul Jackson and all the Ministry DJ's. Serial Diva, Kathy Sledge, Gerideau, The Madd Ladds, Yojo Working and all the Ministry artists. The promotions team and everyone else at MoS Headquarters.

Kate O'Rourke. Matt The Clever Jag. Dom Phillips, Andy Pemberton and all at Mixmag. Christophe Demoulin, Damian, Simone, Blanche and all at Slice Promotions. John, Richard 'Fozzie Bear' Foster and Jessica 'Rabbit' at BMP. Roger Dodge, Jim Kelly, Dave the Rave, Tina, Kev, Yarra and Max at 3MV. Heidi at Pioneer. Sue at Pulsar. Bruno at JBL. Jeff and Pippa at PlayStation.

Toni, Jacko, Lizzie, Joyce, Elisia, Dave and all at Masterpiece Mastering. Gem (thanks!), David Vincent, Glen, Kevin and Vinny the poster boys. Paul Fowler at D.J. Ann and Jeff Young at Young and Dangerous. Scott Murphy and Frank Gee at Mushroom. Marcel and Wally at PIAS. Julie, Chris, Maria and all at Sound Performance. London Fancy Box Co. Karen, Lucy, Natalie and

Amy at Polygram. Paul at Deconstruction UK and US. Tina and Roseann at Zomba Rhythm UK. Simon at Azuli. Lucy at Jazzy Soul at Champion. Brian at Soulfuric, Grant and Kate at Swing City. Kai at Cr Sangki and Tee at Freetown. Scott and

---

Funky Green Dogs
Fired Up!
Murk Vocal

Ralph Falcon. Murk Publishing.
℗ 1996 MCA Records
by arrangement with Twisted.
Produced and mixed by
Ralph Falcon and Oscar Gaetan.

Fonda Rae
Living In Ecstasy (I Like What You Do)
Groove Mix

Lem Springsteen / Fonda Rae.
Moody Black Keys (BMI) / Freetown Music.
℗ 1996 Freetown Inc. Ltd.
Produced and arranged by John Ciafone
and Lem Springsteen.

Giselle Jackson
Love Commandments
Vocal Mix

L. Guzman / W. Turnipseed / P. Turnipseed.
Out Of Order Music / Fairwood Music Ltd.
℗ 1996 Waako Records Inc. Produced, mixed
and edited by Louie 'Balo' Guzman.

The Mighty Dub Katz
Just Another Groove
Original Mix

The Pizzaman.
℗ 1996 Southern Fried Records under
exclusive license to London Records 90 Ltd.
Produced by Andy Mac, G-Money and The Pizzaman.
Courtesy of Polygram Licensing Division.

DJ Sneak
Keep On Groovin'

C. Sosa.
Jessica Michael Music Inc. /
Tip Toe Publishing (ASCAP)
℗ 1996 Strictly Rhythm Records Inc.
Produced and mixed by DJ Sneak.
Licensed courtesy of Strictly Rhythm, U

Federation X
Odyssey One

Grant Nelson / Mousse T.
Wyze Music / Peppermint Park / BMG / UFA.
℗ 1996 Wyze Music / Peppermint Park / BMG / UFA.
under exclusive license to Swing City.
Produced by Grant Nelson & Mousse T.

The Zoo Experience
Presents Over Joyd
Just Follow The Vibe
Vocal Mix

R. Laviniere / S. Laviniere / D. Ellington
Westbury Music / Klub Zoo Int. Music.
Produced and mixed by Bobbi & Steve &
Dave Ellington for Zoo Productions.
℗ 1996 Klub Zoo

M&S Presents The Guy Next Door
Deeper
Epic Klub Mix

R. Morrison / F. Sidoli.
℗ 1996 Strictly Rhythm Records Inc.
Produced and mixed by
Ricky Morrison and Fran Sidoli.
Licensed courtesy of Strictly Rhythm, UK.

Kristine W
Land Of The Living
Deep Dish Vocal

Rob D / Rollo / Kristine W.
BMG / Champion Music.
℗ 1996 Champion Records Ltd.
Produced by Rollo and Rob D.

Re-Vibe-All
The Feeling

Brian Tappert.
℗ 1996 Soulfuric Music.
Produced and arranged by Brian Tappe

East 57th Street
Saturday
Soulfuric Du

Edwards / Roger / Cotter.
℗ 1996 A&M Records Ltd, London.
Produced and mixed by Julian Jonah,
Marco Funari and Mark Hughes.

Danny J. Lewis
I Just Can't Stop

Danny J. Lewis.
℗ 1996 Assured Ltd.
Produced by Danny J. Lewis.

Lovebeads feat. Courtney Grey
This Is The Only Way
Heller and Farley Project Mix

Jahkey B, C Grey. All tracks written by Jahkey B
and Courtney Grey. Produced by Jahkey B
for Above Love Music. Remixed by Terry Farley
and Pete Heller. Published by Artificial Music
(ASCAP) / Above Love Music (ASCAP).
℗ 1997 Ministry Of Sound Recordings Ltd.

Lovebeads feat. Courtney Grey
This Is The Only Way
Mount Rushmore's Superfly Interpretation

All details as previous track, except:
Additional production and remix by
Mount Rushmore for XL Talent.
Engineered by Metal Mickey Mulligan.
℗ 1997 Ministry Of Sound Recordings Ltd.

Deluxe & Simmonds feat. Bo
Peace Of Mind
Barheads Dub

T. Liken, M. Burrel, R Windross. All track
written and produced by Tim Deluxe a
Chris Simmonds. Keyboards Eddie Pa
Bass Guitar Billy Cobham. Engineered
mixed by Howard Bargoff at Rollover Su
℗ 1997 Ministry Of Sound Recordings

Criminal Element Orchestra
Go Around

A. Baker / M. De-Peyer / D. Hall / S. Allen
Shakin' Baker Music / De-Peyer Music /
Unichappell Music / Hit Cha Music.
℗ 1996 4th & Broadway / Island Records.
Produced and mixed by Arthur Baker and Merc De-Peyer.
Courtesy of Polygram Licensing Division.

Mousse T
Everybody

Mousse T.
℗ 1996 BMG / UFA.
Mousse T. BMG / UFA under exclusive
license to Swing City.
Produced by Mousse T.

House Of Glass
feat. Judy Albanese
Take Me Over
FOS Mix

G.Bini, F.Perniola, P.Martini, M. Davies.
FOS Music (SIAE) / U.Jam Music. Produced.
Arranged and mixed by Gianni Bini,
Fulvio Perniola and Paolo Martini.
℗ 1997 Ministry of Sound Recordings Ltd.

Roy Davis Jr.
Symphonic Night

Roy Davis Jr./Umosia (ASCAP).
Produced and mixed by Roy Davis Jr.
Taken from the Powerplant Revisited EP.
℗ 1996 Chord 44 / Container Distribution.
Hamburg, Germany.

Serial Diva
Keep Hope Alive
Burning Diva Mix

Written by Serial Diva / Ann Saunderso
Published by Serial Diva / Ann Saunders
Produced by Serial Diva for DEF.
Mixed and engineered by Tom Frederic
℗ + © 1997 Ministry Of Sound Recordie

SESSIONS SEVEN
MIXED BY DAVID MORALES

OVERLEAF

 A SCOTT PARKER

D SCOTT PARKER,
   THOMAS LARDNER:
   SOUND DESIGN

✪ BEACH:
   DOI-OING

● OPEN RECORDS

P BEN JENNINGS

■ RECORD SLEEVE,
   RECORD
   305 x 305 MM
   12 x 12 IN

✈ UK

Sound Design and Art Direction:
Scott at Ministry.
Photography Christophe Demoulin.

Heep Bros. feat. Sabrena Armstrong
& Barbara Tucker
Keep On Lovin' You
M&S Funky Klub Mix
Produced by Pino Arduini and Negro.
Remixed by Ricky Morrison and Fran Sidoli.
℗ 1996 Azuli Records.

Black Science Orchestra
Save Us
Funky Music
Beedle / Tommy D / Classen / Woolford.
Chrysalis Music / Copyright Control.
℗ 1996 Junior Recordings Ltd.
Produced and arranged by Ashley Beedle
and the Black Science Orchestra.

Urban Blues Project present
Mother Of Pearl feat. Pearlie Mae
Your Heaven
M&S Vocal Epic Klub Mix
Brian Tappert / Marc Pomeroy.
Jazz-N-Groove Music / Paranormal Music.
℗ 1996 Zomba Records Ltd.
Produced by Brian Tappert & Marc Pomeroy

Deep Dish
Stay Gold
Dubfire / Sharam. Copyright Control.
℗ 1996 Deconstruction Ltd.
Produced by Dubfire and Sharam
for Deep Dish Prods.
Licensed courtesy of Deconstruction Ltd.

OF SOUND SSIONS
MIXED BY DAVID MORALES

DOI-OING BEACH REMIXES

OPEN

A	SYNTHLOOP 10	DAVE ANGEL MIX	00.05.37.15
	SYNTHLOOP 10	WINK AND THE LEMMING GETS IT	00.07.53.08
B	SYNTHLOOP 10	SLACK ENVELOPE MIX	00.08.15.75
	SYNTHLOOP 10	DUB MIX	00.05.50.99

OPEN

An Open Minded Collection

A collection of Open minded music for Open minded people. Featuring 20 of the finest tracks from the first two years of Open Records

Features exclusive unreleased tracks from Carl Craig, Paperclip People, K-Hand, Persuasion, + Doi-Oing

Ministry of Sound Presents

◩ SCOTT PARKER:
SOUND DESIGN

✪ AN OPEN MINDED COLLECTION:
VARIOUS ARTISTS

● OPEN RECORDS

ℙ BEN JENNINGS

■ CD COVER, CD, INSIDE OF CD CASE

✈ UK

Disc One Ministry of Sound presents
An Open Minded Collection

All rights of the manufacturer and of the   This compilation
owner of the recorded work reserved.   © 1996 Ministry of Sound Recordings Ltd
Unauthorised public performance,   © 1996 Ministry of Sound Recordings Ltd
broadcasting and copying of this work
prohibited. Made in England.   **OPENCD1**

Disc Two Ministry of Sound presents
An Open Minded Collection

All rights of the manufacturer and of the   This compilation
owner of the recorded work reserved.   © 1996 Ministry of Sound Recordings Ltd
Unauthorised public performance,   © 1996 Ministry of Sound Recordings Ltd
broadcasting and copying of this work
prohibited. Made in England   **OPENCD1**

Open would like to thank all of the artists and
remixers who have contributed to this album
and into making Open what it is today.

We would also like to thank Chris and Martin @ White
Noise. Luke, Nicky and everyone @ Phuture Trax. Mario
and Sharon @ Amato, Damien, Simone and Adam @
Slice PR, Howard and Sean @ Vital Distribution. John,
Pauline and everyone @ Whitfield Street and all the
DJ's and record shops worldwide who have supported
the label over the last 2 years.

Label A&R and Album co-ordination - Jim Masters
Management, Marketing and Production :
Lynn Cosgrave, Mark Rodol, and Steve Canueto
Mastered by John 'The Master' Davies.

■ SCOTT PARKER,
  SOUND DESIGN

✪ GRACE:
  DAN K

● OPEN RECORDS

■ RECORD SLEEVE
  305 X 305 MM
  12 X 12 IN

◨ SMILE

✪ GIVIN' ME LUV:
JNX

● SMILE

■ RECORD SLEEVE
254 x 254 MM
10 x 10 IN

✈ USA

161

Blue Note hi hat

The Blue Note's Sunday Social returns after it's summer break. Downstairs.
The UK's only traditional Jazz dance session. DJ's Latin legend Snowboy and Jonny Kango kick in
with the Latin Fusion and Be-Bop, playing an infectious blend of old skool classics and
Afro rhythms along with the latest real Jazz CD cuts. Re-launches Sunday 27 October.
Every Sunday 1pm-6pm £3 @ The Blue Note, 1 Hoxton Square, London N1 6NU, T: 0171 729 8440

PREVIOUS SPREAD

D HEIWID,
LOPETZ:
BÜRO DESTRUCT

① ★ SMELLY
■ PROMOTIONAL POSTER
420 x 297 MM
16 ½ x 11 ¾ IN

D M. BRUNNER:
BÜRO DESTRUCT

② ★ 100% GROOVE
■ CATALOGUE SPREAD
340 x 240 MM
16 ½ x 13 ⅜ IN
✈ SWITZERLAND

Blue Note cancer research **campaign**

proceeds going to cancer research

pearl

saturday 29 june 10 pm-5 am £6 b4 11 £8 after

3 floors of pure soulful grooves:
main room: the surgery - 70's-2000 mod soul /boogie classics
ground floor: 60's /northen soul
gallery: rare soul and two step

the night will feature dj's from across the uk: bob jones, c j,
graham ellis, bob jefferies, ivor jones, max reese, daddy bug,
stevie cee, miss browning and terry jones

witness this totally unique night of 3 decades of 100% soul
under one roof - the first of its kind in london

a soulful tribute to shirl 'the pearl' wilcox.
the blue note 1 hoxton square london n1 6nu
telephone 0171 729 8440

**SOUL POWER

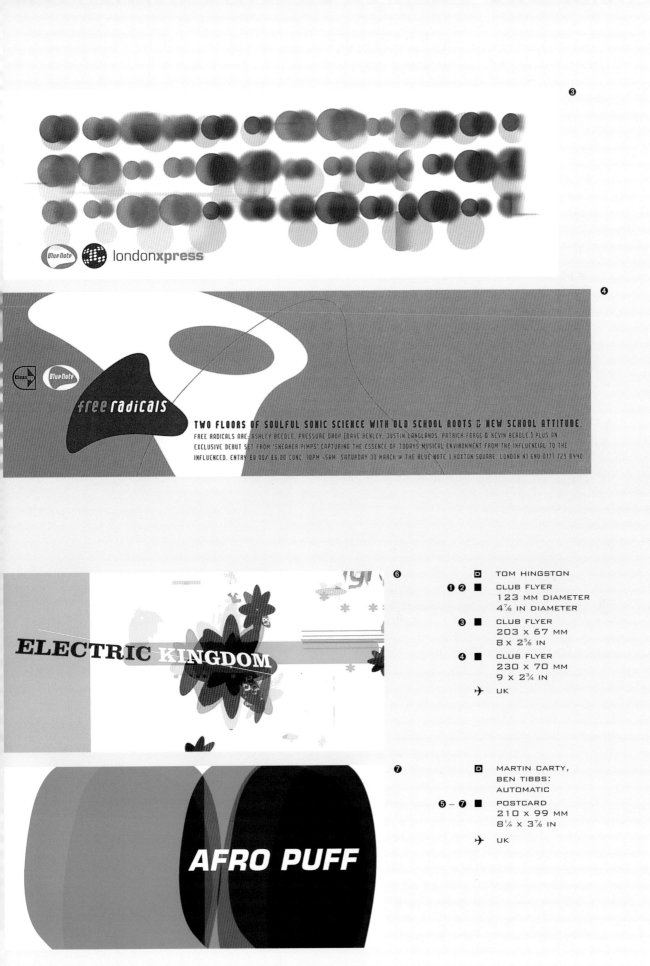

③

Blue Note ⬤ london**xpress**

④

Clean Up · Blue Note

free radicals

TWO FLOORS OF SOULFUL SONIC SCIENCE WITH OLD SCHOOL ROOTS & NEW SCHOOL ATTITUDE.
FREE RADICALS ARE: ASHLEY BEEDLE, PRESSURE DROP (DAVE HENLEY, JUSTIN LANGLANDS, PATRICK FORGE & KEVIN BEADLE.) PLUS AN
EXCLUSIVE DEBUT SET FROM 'SNEAKER PIMPS', CAPTURING THE ESSENCE OF TODAYS MUSICAL ENVIRONMENT FROM THE INFLUENCIAL TO THE
INFLUENCED. ENTRY £8.00/ £6.00 CONC. 10PM -5AM SATURDAY 30 MARCH ⊕ THE BLUE NOTE 1 HOXTON SQUARE, LONDON N1 6NU 0171 729 8440

⑥

ELECTRIC KINGDOM

⑦

AFRO PUFF

⑥	▣	TOM HINGSTON
❶❷	■	CLUB FLYER
		123 MM DIAMETER
		4⅞ IN DIAMETER
❸	■	CLUB FLYER
		203 x 67 MM
		8 x 2⅝ IN
❹	■	CLUB FLYER
		230 x 70 MM
		9 x 2¾ IN
	✈	UK
⑦	▣	MARTIN CARTY,
		BEN TIBBS:
		AUTOMATIC
❺–❼	■	POSTCARD
		210 x 99 MM
		8¼ x 3⅞ IN
	✈	UK

(ri'pub'lika)

Logotype 2

(CDFP)CoolFluorescent(DanceProduct)
Flyer Format No.1 & On-Line

Republica
RepublicaVirtualClubscape®BulletinFeb1997
Bakers Dance Club For The New Millennium / Birmingham / Resident DJ's Scott Bond Andy Cleeton

DECADENCE.ALLNIGHTER>>
SUNDAY 30 MARCH 1997. 10-6AM.
JEREMY HEALY. MARK MOORE. SEB FONTAINE
CRAIG CAMPBELL.LEE FISHER.
BAKERS.BIRMINGHAM.

Bakers 162 Broad St.Birmingham 0121 633 3839.
Coach parties or guest list contact Jo 0631 333963.

40394. Freestyle Records Worcester 01905 619069.Jago Hereford 01432 354451.Joplins Nottingham 0115 950 0765.Music Junction Merry Hill 01384 481128.Network Clothing Stafford 01785
211393.Revive Coventry 01203 336696.Upfront Sutton Coldfield 0121 321 3843.

Decadence™

Bank Holiday Allnighter (10pm-6am)
Sunday 7 April, Bakers

DJs.
Alex P/Tom Wainwright
Craig Campbell/Jules Verne/Lee Fisher

Tickets: £10.00, more on the door.
Outlets: Bakers The Club (B'ham) 0121 633 3839. Autograph(B'ham) 0121 633 3540.
Depot(B'ham) 0121 643 6045. Fatrat Records(Kingswinford) 01384 400511. Freestyle
Records(Worcester) 01905 619069. Upfront Clothing(Sutton Coldfield) 0121 321 3843.
Bakers The Club, 162 Broad Street, Birmingham. Tel: (0121) 633 3839.

RICHARD HUNT,
SCOTT RAYBOULD:
Z3 ASSOCIATES

■ CLUB FLYER
210 x 99 MM
8¼ x 3⁷⁄₈ IN

✈ UK

▣ JON FORSS,
  SIMON MAY:
  MAY THE FORSS...

❷ ❹ ℗ JON FORSS

❶ – ❸ ■ CLUB FLYER
  210 x 74 MM
  8 ¼ x 2 ⅛ IN

❹ ■ MAGAZINE ADVERTISEMENT
  228 x 279 MM
  9 x 11 IN

✈ UK

❶

❷

❸

Derek Ba
iley vs
The Ruin
us Room
(Guitar/Drums&Bass)

Cor
nershop
(+SpecialG
uest)

HEART OV THE BASS

tuesday november 12th

heart ov the bass

kicking the beatz to the heart ov the bass and beyond!!

wedNesdAy 2nd octOber

luke vibert
(wagon christ)

For the month of October a night ov exquisite lunar beats and spaced driven bass to take you out there into the realms ov the night to escape the autumn chill.

★ignition

musik pre s e ntS a showcas e Of live un d e Rground drum & bass

lIve **p.a.** by kaleiDoscope

resident: dj pants

not just drum & bass

doors 10pm-2am   £4 / £3 concs
@ the concorde, madeira drive, brighton

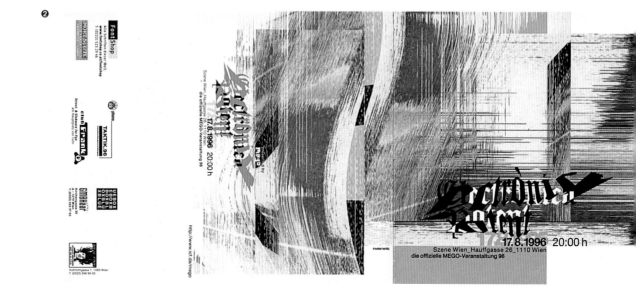

Szene Wien_Hauffgasse 26_1110 Wien
die offizielle MEGO-Veranstaltung 96

17.8.1996 20:00 h

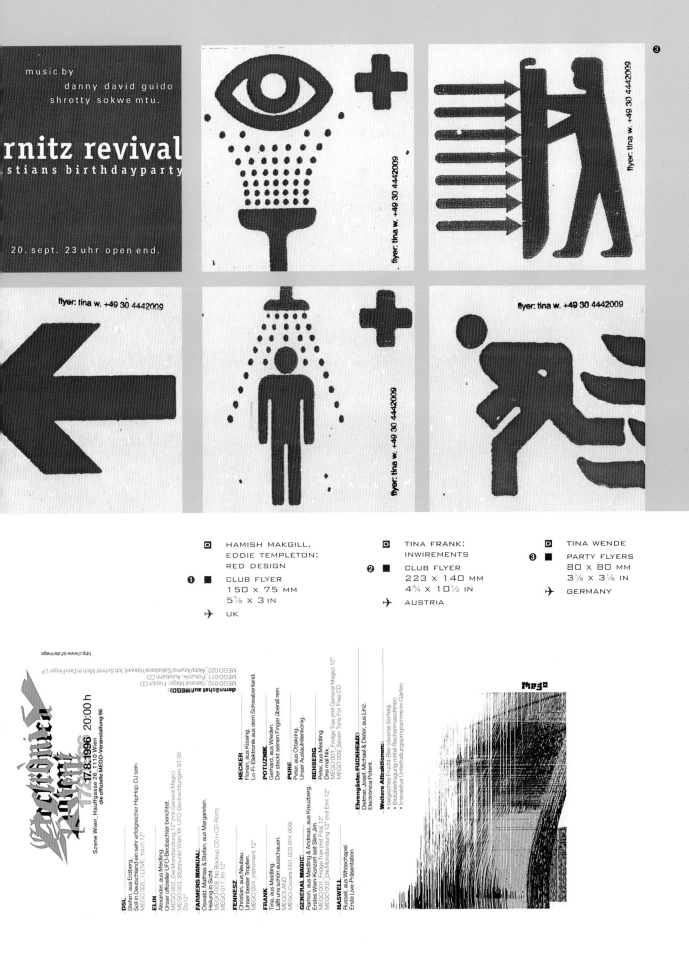

music by
danny david guido
shrotty sokwe mtu.

rnitz revival
stians birthdayparty

20. sept. 23 uhr open end.

flyer: tina w. +49 30 4442009

▣ HAMISH MAKGILL,
   EDDIE TEMPLETON:
   RED DESIGN
❶ ■ CLUB FLYER
     150 x 75 MM
     5⅞ x 3 IN
   ✈ UK

▣ TINA FRANK:
   INWIREMENTS
❷ ■ CLUB FLYER
     223 x 140 MM
     4¾ x 10½ IN
   ✈ AUSTRIA

▣ TINA WENDE
❸ ■ PARTY FLYERS
     80 x 80 MM
     3⅛ x 3⅛ IN
   ✈ GERMANY

❶

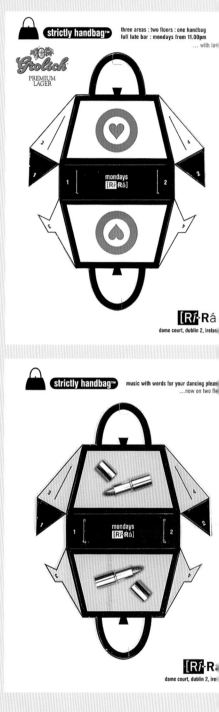

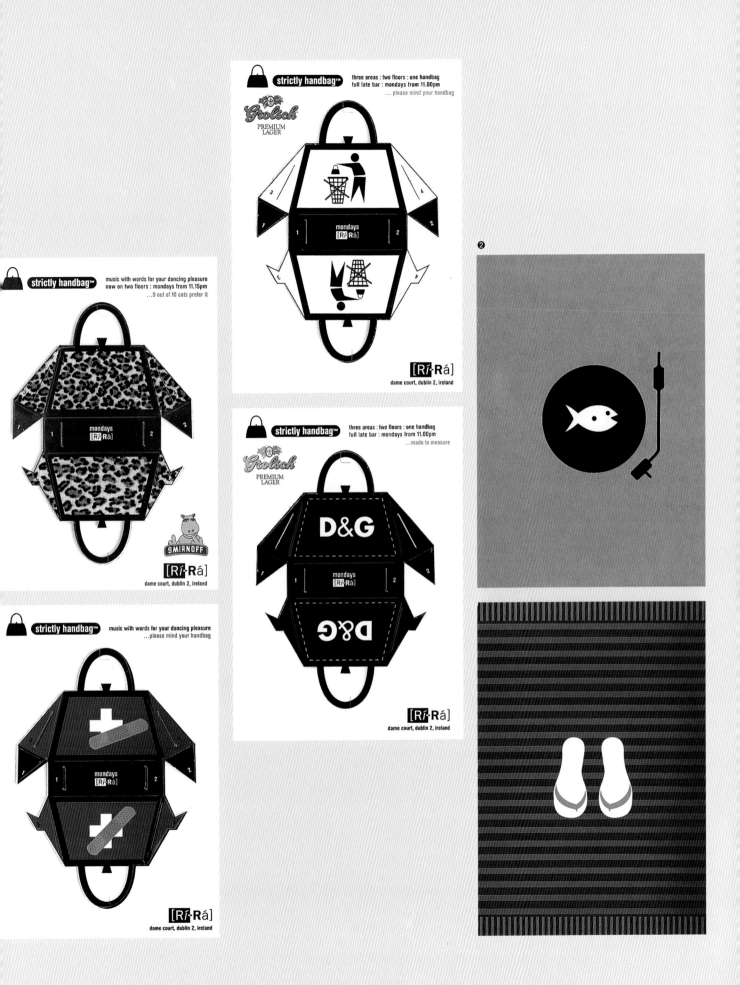

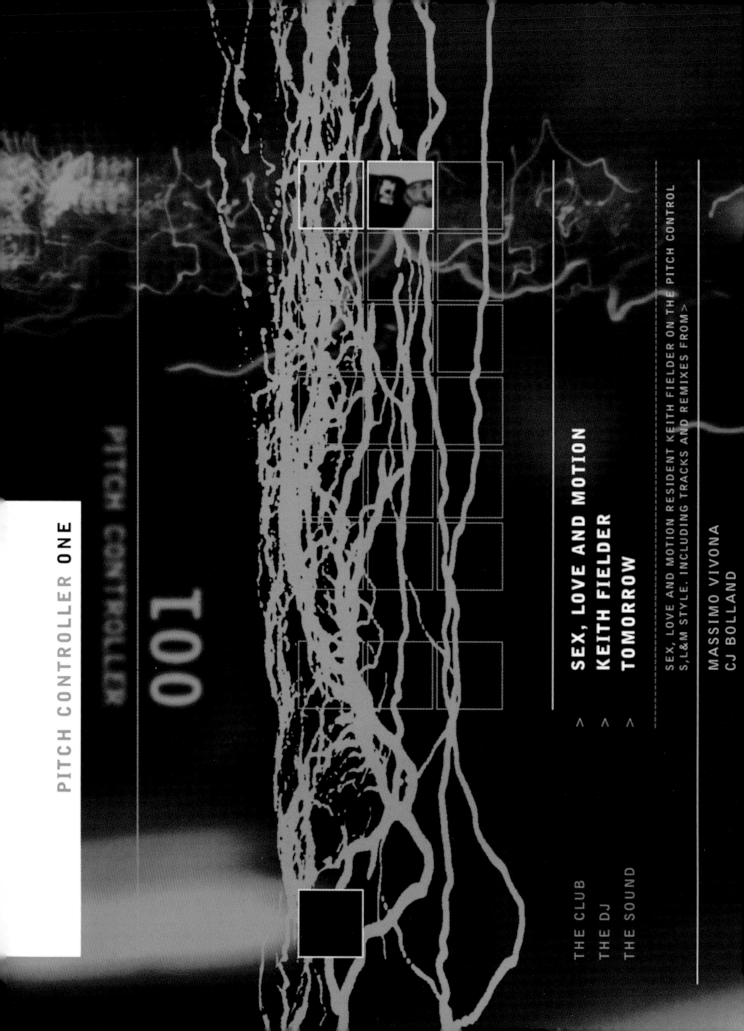

PITCH CONTROLLER ONE

PITCH CONTROLLER

001

THE CLUB   > SEX, LOVE AND MOTION
THE DJ   > KEITH FIELDER
THE SOUND   > TOMORROW

SEX, LOVE AND MOTION RESIDENT KEITH FIELDER ON THE PITCH CONTROL
S,L&M STYLE. INCLUDING TRACKS AND REMIXES FROM>

MASSIMO VIVONA
CJ BOLLAND

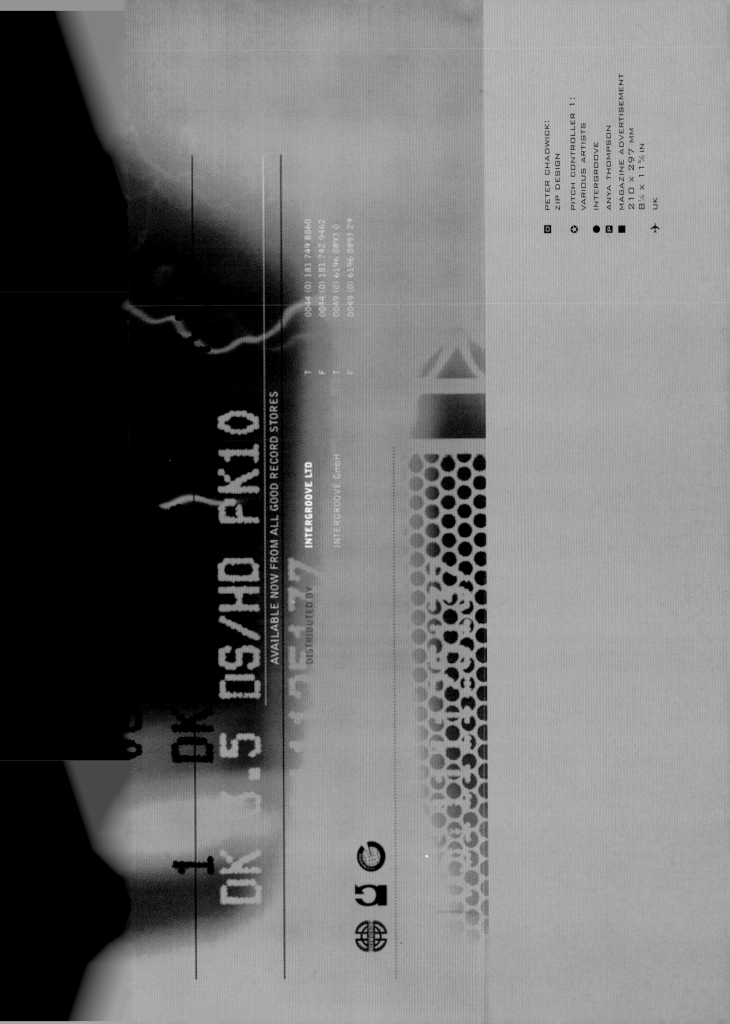

DK 3.5 DS/HD PK10

AVAILABLE NOW FROM ALL GOOD RECORD STORES

DISTRIBUTED BY **INTERGROOVE LTD**

T 0044 (0) 181 749 8860
F 0044 (0) 181 742 9462

INTERGROOVE GmbH

T 0049 (0) 6196 8893 0
F 0049 (0) 6196 8893 29

PETER CHADWICK:
ZIP DESIGN

PITCH CONTROLLER 1:
VARIOUS ARTISTS

INTERGROOVE

ANYA THOMPSON

MAGAZINE ADVERTISEMENT
210 X 297 MM
8¼ X 11¾ IN

UK

MINISTRY OF SOUND
APRIL LISTINGS 1997
NEUTRICK CONNECTOR

(ⓝ) NEUTRIK

HUNDREDS OF CONNECTORS LINK THE
MILES OF CABLE THAT JOIN THE
COMPONENTS OF MINISTRY OF
SOUND'S SOUND SYSTEM. WE INSIST
ON USING NEUTRICK CONNECTORS, IN
PARTICULAR THE XLR CATEGORY, THE
FINEST IN THE WORLD. 3,4,5,8 AND 7

PIN CONFIGURATIONS THROUGHOUT
THE SYSTEM WITH FEATURES LIKE
FOUR-PART CONSTRUCTION USING A
SCREW-ON 'BOOT' AND A
COMPRESSIONS GLAND CHUCK. THIS
ENSURES SECURE STRAIN RELIEF ON
CABLES FROM 2.8MM TO 8.0MM

DIAMETER AND GIVES EXCELLENT
PROTECTION AGAINST BEND STRESS
ON THE CONTACTS, THUS
PREVENTING FAILURE. YET MORE
ATTENTION TO DETAIL THAT ADDS TO
THE LEGEND THAT IS THE MINISTRY'S
SOUND SYSTEM.

❶

Ⓓ SCOTT PARKER:
　 SOUND DESIGN

❶ ■ CLUB FLYER
　 148 × 210 MM
　 5⅞ × 8¼ IN

❷❸ ■ CLUB FLYER
　 105 × 150 MM
　 4⅛ × 5⅞ IN

✈ UK

❶ ▶ RON FAAS,
MICHIEL DE WREEDE:

❷ ❸ ▶ TIRSO FRANCÉS:
DIETWEE ONTWERPERS

❶ – ❸ ■ CLUB FLYER
223 x 140 MM
8¾ x 5½ IN

✈ THE NETHERLANDS

❶

❷

❸

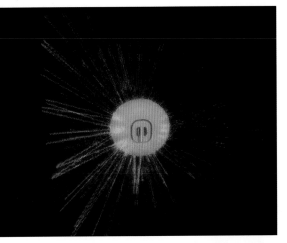

LEFT, ABOVE AND FOLLOWING SPREAD

▣ HEIWID,
LOPETZ:
BÜRO DESTRUCT

✪ CONTEXT

● VIRUS, KUNSTOFF-AREAL, SOLOTHURN

Ⓟ HANDYCAM: CASPAR MARTIG

■ VIDEO STILLS FOR A DISCUSSION AND PARTY
736 x 580 PIXELS

✈ SWITZERLAND

LEFT AND ABOVE

▣ HEIWID,
LOPETZ:
BÜRO DESTRUCT

✪ FSOZ: FUTURE SOUND OF ZURICH

● ENERGETIC RECORDS

Ⓟ HANDYCAM: CAFÉ MÉLANGE

■ VIDEO STILLS FOR A CD LAUNCH PARTY
736 x 580 PIXELS

✈ SWITZERLAND